A Practical Libertarian

A Roadmap to Recovering Liberty

JAMES TALL

A Practical Libertarian

A Practical Libertarian
Copyright © 2019 by James Tall

Edited by Lynn Tall, Edie Tall, Harvey Tall and Ed Schwartz

Cover photo by license from Shutterstock

All rights reserved. No part of this book may be reproduced or transmitted in any form or by any means without written permission from the author, except for the use of quotations in a book review.

ISBN 9781075614576

Library of Congress Control Number:2019944453

A PRACTICAL LIBERTARIAN
A Roadmap to Recovering Liberty

Fierce independence and a 'leave me alone' attitude define the modern Libertarian and party. This does not make for good politics where coordination and national momentum is crucial. This book outlines a practical libertarianism that can coexist with the two other national parties. We CAN find a common, central philosophy that will capture the drive of an election-winning majority of 'We the People'.

James Tall,
A Practical Libertarian

A Practical Libertarian

Prologue: What is a Libertarian?

Libertarianism is a political philosophy that closely identifies with that of the US Founders. "Belief in personal liberty, economic freedom, and a skepticism of government power"[1] as stated by one libertarian group is a good start, but it only brushes the surface of what it really means.

At its heart is the profound prominence of individual rights. As in our Declaration of Independence: "They are endowed by their Creator with certain unalienable Rights". Those unalienable rights are not granted by government, but by something higher (our Creator) that Governments cannot change, take, or usurp.

The founding documents – the Declaration of Independence, the Constitution of the United States, and the Bill of Rights – are held in the highest esteem by most Libertarians and embody the guiding principles of the Party and members. They are flawed by what we now understand are some unseemly customs of the times, but all in all they have given the US an abundance of prosperity and unprecedented longevity for a single modern government.

The rights these documents enumerate can be succinctly described as having all control and freedom of your person as long as your actions do not impede the rights of another. Therefore, the proper purpose of Government is simply to protect the rights of the People. Protection from violence and fraud, and from forces that would limit those rights.

The Constitution lays out the powers of Government as initially described in the Declaration of Independence. Notice, I said 'lays out the powers' and not 'lays out the limitations'. There are simple and few enumerated powers and it was highly intentional that government was to serve limited purposes and not take on the task du jour that was popular.

We've strayed from this intention. Government regularly pushes the bounds of the constitution and has lost the historical context for phrases like 'the general welfare'.

---

[1] https://theihs.org/who-we-are/what-is-libertarian/

A Practical Libertarian

We've evolved our government into one that holds its own people in contempt. It is intrusive in our daily lives, it doesn't think we're smart enough to do things for ourselves or be in charge of our own behaviors. Government (it's agencies and their career employees) and politicians believe they know better how to build wealth, create employment, and plan our retirements. Government wants to be the central pillar of our lives; a new religion.

It was never intended that Government would create and enforce laws controlling what medications we could ingest, requiring government permission; what foods we could eat, with or without permission[2]. It was never intended Government would control how we save for retirement, or that we would give away control of those savings. In fact, you would be hard pressed, if you include state and local government, to find something that you can do without government permission at all, these days. A recent exchange on social media discussed that subject where someone said 'You're free to cross the street'. The curt reply was 'as long as you're in the crosswalk'.

If you boil this down, what you find in a Libertarian is someone who believes that they are responsible for their own self, their own destiny, and is willing to take the risks along with the rewards that come with that. This is the essence of liberty and the foundation upon which this country was built.

---

[2] Think raw milk and raw milk cheeses, CBD oil, or in what proportions foods served in schools were mandated.

Contents

A PRACTICAL LIBERTARIAN iii
Prologue: What is a Libertarian? v
   Contents vii
Introduction 1
Symptoms of Our Broken System 4
   We Have Lost Control of the State 4
   Division Creates Power 8
   Government is Force 12
   Winners and Losers 14
   Social Collision 15
   Moral Hazard 18
   'Entangling Alliances' 22
   Markets 23
   Market Protection 24
   Regulation of Everything 25
   No one is Watching the Watchers 26
   The Pandering Drive to Socialism 28
   Spending 31
   Rights and Responsibilities 33
   Symptoms Summarized 34
Libertarians and Factions 35
   Why 'Practical Libertarianism' 37
Common Ground 46
   Right: 46
   Left: 47
   Center: 47

Practical Steps to do Today to Start Turning the Ship 49
    Have Ground Rules 49
    Respect Opinion 51
    Separate People from Corporations 51
    Implement the 'Fair Tax' 52
    Fix Immigration 55
    Medical Bill of Rights 57
    Campaign Finance Reform 60
    Enact Election Reform 61
    Have a Legal Do-over 62
Conclusion 64

Introduction

We live in very uncomfortable political times. It is perhaps second only to the 'war between the states' that we are so very polarized.

What makes this polarization so alarming now, is the lack of civility. Not only do people not listen to each other, not only do they ignore questions and speak in the *sound bite* that they have been programmed to repeat (think 'talking points'), but they use their polarized positions like a weapon.

Politicians and news commentators come out of their corners, throw a jab and run back where they get back slaps from supporters. They're never fully engaged. There's no back and forth in the spar: no opportunity to teach, no opportunity to learn.

If you repeat something enough it becomes truth. When CNN repeatedly asks politicians questions based on a misleading premise the implication becomes truth regardless of how misplaced it is. Media watchdogs have rated them 'Left' saying, "CNN typically utilizes loaded emotional words in sensational headlines..."[3]

Before you call me a 'neocon' for calling out CNN, Fox and others do the same on the other side... the same organization calls "Fox News strongly Right-Biased due to wording and story selection that favors the right and mixed factually based on poor sourcing"

> "One of the most sincere forms of respect is actually listening to what another has to say." --Bryant H. McGill

Following politics years ago I was fascinated by Tip O'Neil, the Massachusetts US Representative who became Speaker of the House. We weren't on the same page politically, but he spoke with conviction and had my respect. Unlike many of today's partisans on both sides, I felt like he had given the issues thought. It's ok that we ended up on opposite sides, we came to our conclusions naturally.

He could be partisan during the day, but it was famously quipped that he and President Reagan were friends after 6pm. Their partisanship led to a record number of government shutdowns, but in the end, they didn't seem to let their

---

3 https://mediabiasfactcheck.com/cnn/

political differences turn their personal relationship bitter and they agreed and cooperated quite a bit on foreign policy.

If one can read past the negativity in the body politic, and in the media reporting it, you find that people aren't far apart in what they want. Most people want to be left alone. Most people just want a fair shake. They're willing to pay for reasonable government services, but they expect their management to be efficient and cost sensitive, and not give any *one* group advantages.

So, how do we do that? How do we identify all the ways that we can get along, and identify all the political beliefs that we share? And, mute the exploitive, combative language designed to separate us?

I believe that a libertarian centric philosophy of equal opportunity, of fairness, of individualism, is the path that can return 'we the people' to a people of success.

If we can get people to listen.

Listening is a tough thing. It means setting aside some of your confidence, some of your 'I'm right' machismo, to admit that someone else might be 'righter'. To really listen to an opposing view requires you to take another look at something you've probably reinforced in your head, and with your political clan, to the point of blind belief.

The extremism that we see in politics is destructive. The extreme Left's economic socialism and international imperialism, the extreme Right's rigid social doctrine and international imperialism, and the Libertarian extreme's anarchy all present unsustainable, dangerous philosophies.

What I hope to communicate in this document is a center, practical libertarian philosophy taking the economic freedoms touted by the right, the social freedoms touted by the left and the rugged individualism touted by the Libertarians.

Let's start with a frank discussion about where we are and the symptoms of our current, broken system. We'll touch on the libertarian philosophy, specifically, because it's greatly misunderstood. Then we'll review the center's common ground with each party and where we differ. Right, Left, Libertarian.

Finally, we'll discuss steps we can take to start steering this ship of state back towards freedom, and what a center, practical libertarian government and society would look like. This in the context of how it addresses the ills that we've identified.

The views I espouse here are mine and not a mainstream libertarian view or any other '...ian' or '...ism' view. The terms 'left' and 'right' refer generally to the Democratic and Republican party, respectively, but are used more generally to the collective groups even within the parties. The Libertarian Party is similarly generalized as the spectrum of views from mine to anarchist covers a broad swath[4].

Just a note about the oddities of English. The Libertarian Party is spelled with a capital L and the philosophy with a lower-case l. The line is sometimes fuzzy where the philosophy and party merge so I apologize if the cases don't always make this clear.

It is not intended that this book cover every little issue, but it is my hope that this will serve as a conversation starter. A mental time out to say 'hey, we're not that different', and open dialog to organize in a productive, not destructive manner.

---

[4] Like the left and right, the Libertarians include a range of viewpoints from mine to minarchist, anarchist, anarcho-capitalist and egalitarian. If you're not familiar with these please take a moment to look them up, I will not define them further here.

Symptoms of Our Broken System

We can't begin to discuss fixing our system of government without first identifying our starting point.

We Have Lost Control of the State

The preamble to our constitution says "We the People of the United States... establish this Constitution..." *The People* are creating the groundwork for their government and the rules under which it must live. This was a huge triumph at the time, when kings and emperors ruled, for *The People* to determine how they wanted to be governed.

Fast forward 240 years and see what has developed from that original plan:

- Many freedoms, that we told the government in the constitution and bill of rights were inalienable, are violated regularly: violations of the 1st, 2nd, 4th, 5th, 8th, 10th amendments. They are under siege regularly.
- Congress regularly exempts itself from the laws it passes for the People
- Governments at all levels, Federal, State and Municipal, have undertaken spending and spending commitments that they have not accounted for in income. This is evident not only in the annual federal deficit, but in the state's and many city's underfunded pensions and crumbling infrastructure.
- Those whom we have trusted to manage our affairs have violated the principles under which we created our government by creating entangling alliances and allowing us to get sucked into regional and foreign conflicts where we have no business, and where there is no clear ally.

Let's break these out and look at them in some more detail.

1st Amendment:

Free speech and press violations are perpetually in the courts with mixed results as they work their way through the state and federal systems.

In a recent case the Supreme Court remanded a case where someone was arrested as a way to silence their speech. Judge Gorsuch made some interesting comments:

> *In our own time and place, criminal laws have grown so exuberantly and come to cover so much previously innocent conduct that almost anyone can be arrested for something. If the state could use these laws not for their intended purposes but to silence those who voice unpopular ideas, little would be left of our First Amendment liberties, and little would separate us from the tyrannies of the past or the malignant fiefdoms of our own age. The freedom to speak without risking arrest is "one of the principal characteristics by which we distinguish a free nation." -- Justice Neil Gorsuch, dissenting, Nieves v. Bartlett (2019)*

And, the persecution of Wikileaks' Assange has chilled reporters who routinely expose misdeeds in similar ways to how Assange exposed massive spying by our government. He is being persecuted because he embarrassed the government by calling out their misdeeds.

Freedom of the Press and Speech grant us the ability to manage our government and without them we cannot make sound judgments on who to elect.

2nd Amendment:

Violations of gun rights with Massachusetts style restrictions on weapons that aren't on the 'approved firearms roster' make a joke of the phrase 'Shall not be infringed'.

Washington DC used to have an outright ban on handguns which was found unconstitutional in DC v Heller. So did Chicago.

Continued 2nd amendment challenges go on, most recently with 'New York State Rifle & Pistol Association v. New York City' where the City of NY seems to think they can prevent you from traveling outside of the city with a weapon that is registered there. This is regardless of whether you have a residence, or belong to a shooting range or club. It's hard to know how this should be thrown out: under the 2nd amendment for overstepping control of firearms, or for violating the implicit right to travel (discussed later on).

Continued debate on gun laws seem to center around the phrase 'a well regulated militia'. Everyone at the time of the founding was subject to being called into the militia. Indeed, even today every male over 17 and under 45 is by default a member of the 'unorganized' militia according to the Militia Act of 1903.

4th Amendment:

Violations of search and seizure laws force people to put their fingers on cell phones to unlock them for inspection without probable cause. They allow spying on you by warrantless inspection of a cell phone carrier's records.

Many states allow civil forfeiture for supposed crimes that you're never charged with, nor convicted of, only based on suspicion.

Some states and cities allow 'stop and frisk' policing where you can be searched seemingly at random.

5th Amendment:

Using force to use your biometrics to unlock cell phones and computers violate your right against self-incrimination. This is in dispute and is working its way through the courts in several places, specifically in the Northern District of California.

Using eminent domain to take property and then sell it for private use when a city doesn't like what you're doing with it, like the Midtown Mall in Worcester, MA is a flagrant violation.

8th Amendment:

Civil asset forfeiture is not only a violation of our 4th amendment rights, but can also be considered 'excessive fines'. There have been some challenges to this lately, but the practice continues.

10th Amendment:

"The powers not delegated to the United States by the Constitution, nor prohibited by it to the States, are reserved to the States respectively, or to the people."

I spell that one out, where I didn't the others, because it's little known. It is the final amendment of the Bill of Rights, and arguably the most important. And, one we ignore.

There are lots of powers we did not delegate to the federal government in the constitution that it now performs. Regulating healthcare, education, standing quasi agencies that underwrite mortgages, agencies that spy on us, our adversaries and allies regardless of our state of war or peace. Agencies that prohibit our travel to foreign lands, a Federal Reserve Bank... As they were not authorized in the constitution, they should not be performed by the United States government.

Congressional Exemption:

Until 1995, Congress was exempt from a number of laws. The Congressional Accountability Act resolved many of these, including much of the Civil Rights Act, the Fair Labor Standards Act, Family and Medical Leave, and the Americans with Disabilities Act.

However, many exemptions remain. Congress does not need to produce information under the Freedom of Information Act, does not protect whistle blowers, and neither has to train employees about their employment rights like they require everyone else, nor do they keep records about their injuries on the job.

Unfunded Future Commitments:

Social Security and Medicare are obvious places to look for unfunded spending. Social Security is a Ponzi scheme that relies on this year's income to support this year's spending. We had a surplus for a very long time, but the Federal Government took it upon itself to use that surplus in the general fund and replace it with an IOU.

Well, that IOU is coming due and we don't have the income to cover expenses starting very soon.

Another unfunded issue are pension plans. In the Federal Government, pseudo governmental agencies like the Post Office, and many states and cities the biggest threat to future budgets are underfunded retirement plans.

The problem is so bad in California that an organization set up a 'pensiontracker.org' website that tracks the Public Employee Pension System (CalPERS). It currently reads (2017 data) a market basis per household net debt of over $78,000. Per HOUSEHOLD.

The top ten according to Forbes.com range from over $58,000 to $102,000 per household.[5] Like Social Security, we've gotten away with this till now because of

---

5 https://www.forbes.com/sites/chuckdevore/2019/05/31/5-2-trillion-of-government-pension-debt-threatens-to-overwhelm-state-budgets-taxpayers/#6150e76a759d

the balance of workers to retirees. As that balance shifts with the retirement of the Baby Boomers these numbers will be insurmountable.

Division Creates Power

In the introduction we touched on the polarity and lack of true communication that have magnified our differences to make them seem insurmountable. Each side does this to make themselves look like they have the correct answer. By magnifying the differences between us we create a sense of urgency to act. After all, if we don't elect an X in this election then the world will end in a global warming explosion, the penguins won't have ice to mate on, and the communists will take over all the businesses!

I don't believe that these differences make up a large part of the political spectrum. They are an imaginary construct built to focus power. When asked in polling about people's political views, a majority would welcome a third party[6], and people agree on a surprisingly large number of issues.

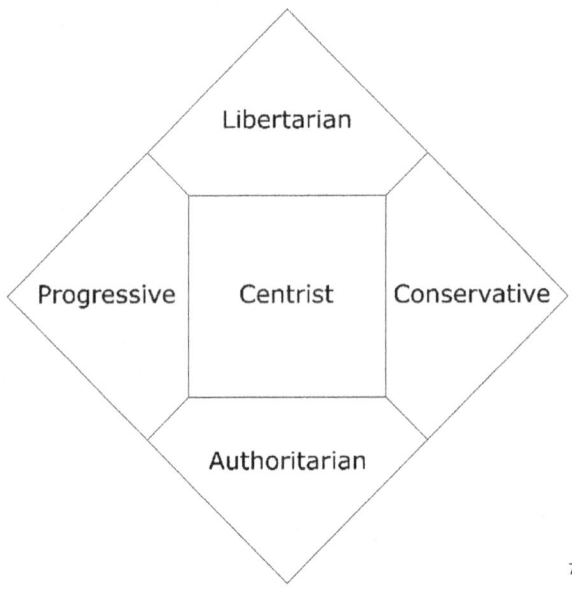

[7]

---

6 https://news.gallup.com/poll/244094/majority-say-third-party-needed.aspx
7 Jay Coop, https://commons.wikimedia.org/wiki/File:Nolan_chart.svg

The draw to division may be innate. "Confirmation Bias" leads us to believe only that which reinforces our beliefs or 'gut instinct'. "...we lack a natural ease in questioning our own ideas or opening our minds up to those that do not mesh with our already-held belief structures."[8] It is difficult to overcome this and the ability to set aside these biases takes practice.

Current social and news media help exploit this by restricting the viewpoints that someone is presented with. If you have a Facebook account and all your 'friends' are of a similar political viewpoint then you will only see posts that confirm and further radicalize your viewpoint.

If you follow a particular news organization (pick CNN or Fox for polar examples) then you will only see articles that reinforce and back up your views making opposing views seem nefarious.

With confirmation bias, news doesn't have to be fake to be misleading. Putting emphasis on only part of an explanation or only calling out facts that help your argument (and, conveniently ignoring others) make news seem like it leans one way.

All sides in the political spectrum exploit the fringes of their philosophies to divide people.

Democrats exploited fear of religious conservatives to keep out a restaurant that is closed on Sundays and made public statements opposing gay marriage. Boston long used zoning laws to keep Chick-Fil-A out of the city, with then Mayor Menino writing the company president telling him to stay out of Boston.

Republicans exploit fear of terrorism to perpetuate and expand mass surveillance. Former Director of National Intelligence McConnell blamed the 9/11 terrorist attacks on 'weak' wiretapping laws.

The one thing that these examples show agreement on is the use of government force to further each group's aims. It's just that each group has different aims.

It's ok to disagree on the outcomes. You don't have to patronize a restaurant that espouses religious views that you don't like. The market will determine its success. After all, if there are enough patrons to keep them open and profitable then who

---

8 https://www.psychologytoday.com/us/blog/moderating/201807/the-psychology-political-division

does this hurt? And, if one restaurant is kept away out of religious zeal then watch out because your choice may be the next target.

It's not ok to violate the 5th amendment with unconstitutional wiretaps just because there was an off chance the one call between terrorists might have been caught.

What we should be agreeing upon is NOT using government to encourage one group's desired behavior. As we've seen since the 2016 election, one President's use of emergency power should not make it ok for the next President's use of emergency power.

President Obama's use of the power that Congress abdicated in creating DACA was just as wrong as President Trumps use of emergency power to redirect funds to build a Mexico border wall. Wouldn't it have been best for Congress to have kept their powers and held public debate?

<u>Beware!</u> Don't take the disagreement with tactic to mean disagreement with the outcome. There are proper ways of achieving both these goals, so please don't 'sound bite' this to imply anything. We'll discuss immigration more fully later in a section about what a Practical Libertarian policy would look like.

Senator and Presidential candidate Bernie Sanders once tweeted "Authoritarians seek power by promoting division and hatred." It was apparently lost on him that the socialism he espouses is the ultimate authoritarianism... government control of *SO* much of the economy... you'll have the health care that we provide, you'll have the retirement plan we provide, you'll have the wage that the government determines is right, regardless of a business's ability to pay it, or the actual value of the labor.

All three sides use this division, because if you think of it, it's the activists that do the most campaigning and most 'activity'... that's why they're called activists!

The Liberals driving the 2020 presidential talking points are pushing government as the answer to all that ails us. Free healthcare, free college tuition, universal basic income.

The Conservatives driving the debate are pushing our status as world policeman with an authoritarian philosophy of threatening war wherever there's a leader who doesn't kowtow. North Korea, Iran, China, Russia all face embargoes or trade sanctions currently, with the aim of having them bend the knee.

A Practical Libertarian

The Libertarians driving the party are the extreme as well... you don't get far in the Libertarian Party if you aren't 'libertarian enough'. One big L with sights on the presidential nomination of the party, Arvin Vohra, is a self-labeled anarchist and says his administration would immediately end the welfare state and abolish public schools. Maybe in an ideal libertarian world, but he never addresses how he'll fit libertarian ideas in a mixed political environment.

None of the parties do. In their book *Wedged,* Fogg and Greene illustrate how the extremes in each party drive the narrative.

The Greene-Fogg curve elegantly illustrates how the bulk of the populace have pretty central views, yet it is the fringes driving debate with their artificial divisiveness.

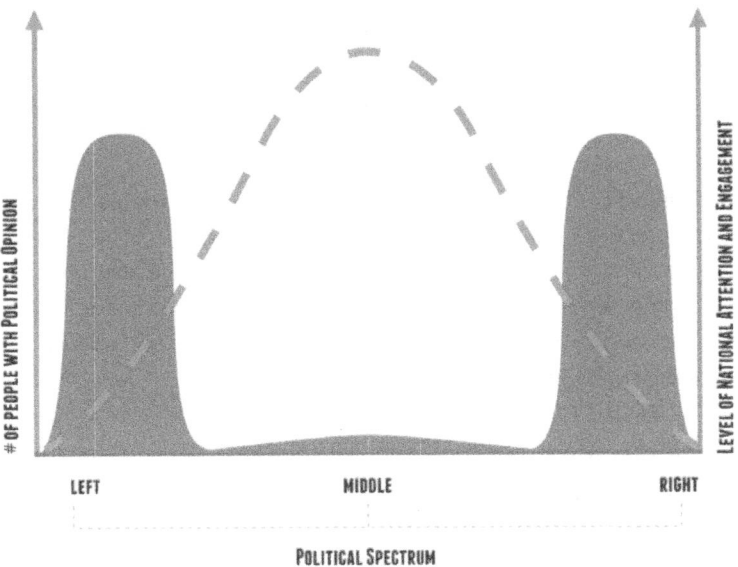

9 https://www.reconsidermedia.com/lastestblogposts/the-greene-fogg-curve-and-presidential-debates

Government is Force

The government has been granted powers 'by the people' to perform tasks on its behalf. The constitution enumerates the powers that the Federal government has. Those powers were very carefully chosen to restrain the government from becoming what the founders had just thrown off: 'repeated injuries and usurpations, all having in direct object the establishment of an absolute Tyranny.'[10]

The founding documents specify that the government is to protect us from invasion (common defense), fraud (establish justice), provide for the 'general welfare', and to do this they may 'lay and collect' taxes.

The General Welfare clause is one that causes a huge amount of confusion. It has been used to justify all kinds of action that it wasn't intended to be used for. It is now used to justify 'specific welfare' for individuals and groups as opposed to 'general' to apply to all.

The phrase 'general welfare' first appeared with better definition in the Articles of Confederation, the predecessor to the Constitution. There it read:

> "All charges of war, and all other expences that shall be incurred for the common defence and _general welfare_, and allowed by the United States in Congress assembled, shall be defrayed out of a common treasury"

In Madison's Report of 1800, he explains the intent of the General Welfare clause. Madison explained the limitations of the general welfare clause by saying that given its prior use, "it will scarcely be said that in the former they were ever understood to be either a general grant of power, or to authorize the requisition or application of money by the old Congress to the common defence and general welfare, except in the cases afterwards enumerated which explained and limited their meaning"[11] In other words, Madison said these were in reference to the government's ability to lay taxes and not to expand on powers that were enumerated specifically.

The government has nothing that it doesn't take from the people by force. There is nothing it regulates, or behavior it outlaws, without the threat or application of force: If you don't pay your income taxes, Government will descend through

---

10 The Declaration of Independence
11 https://tenthamendmentcenter.com/2017/06/05/general-welfare-and-common-defense-explained-by-james-madison/

various punishments ultimately jailing you, taking your freedom. If you don't comply with a law requiring business registration you will face various punishments ultimately ending in imprisonment.

Laws are a bludgeon and should be used sparingly.

It may be that people look to government out of fear. My friend, author and libertarian commentator Adrian Wyllie has very astute observations. He wrote this about government and fear:

> "Support for government is a reaction to fear.
>
> "Conservatives fear others. They fear criminals, immigrants, and anyone outside their social group. They want walls, armies, and law and order. They cling to the security of the majority, as there is safety in numbers, and they demand that government enforces tradition. They need government to protect them.
>
> "Liberals fear themselves. The fear they are unable to provide for their own basic needs. They want guaranteed income, education, transportation, healthcare and housing. They cling to victimhood and oppression to justify their insecurities, and they demand that government enforces equality. They need government to care for them.
>
> "When you realize you can protect and provide for yourself -- and that government causes or perpetuates most of the problems Conservatives and Liberals fear -- you stop being afraid.
>
> When you stop being afraid, you begin to wonder whether we really need government at all." -- Adrian Wyllie

When you merge the politics of division with fear of bad outcomes and submission to force, the fear lets government get away with all kinds of things we wouldn't consider in its absence.

About fear, Robert Higgs wrote, "They [politicians] exploit it, and they cultivate it. Whether they compose a warfare state or a welfare state, they depend on it to secure popular submission, compliance with official dictates, and, on some occasions, affirmative cooperation with the state's enterprises and adventures."[12]

Politicians don't pass bills and gain power with a positive message. The media doesn't sell papers (does anyone read papers anymore? Rephrase to 'adspace'), because the readership is drawn to the negative and the fantastic.

How much do we allow fear of the force of Government to dictate our actions? Do you violate your religious views because of fear of persecution by the state? Do you cower in fear of exaggerated crime statistics or manipulated employment and earnings statistics?

I'm not cowering, and I hope you're not either.

Winners and Losers

When laws are proposed we don't spend time looking at the results of that law: though a positive outcome is desired, one must ask 'who does this affect negatively'.

At the state and local levels, this is easier to demonstrate. 13 states require a cosmetology license to braid hair.[13] For whom is this advantageous? Only hair salons looking to protect their business from competition, or people with racist views on ethnic coiffure.

It certainly doesn't help the consumer. The consumer may or may not like the results of one person's braiding, it doesn't matter if they're licensed or not. It doesn't produce competition that limits price, the licensing does the opposite. It ultimately harms the consumer and potential business owners who don't have the means to enter the protected market.

Neither does licensing guarantee quality. If you don't like the way your hair was braided you can decide not to go back the next time. If something was done that was physically damaging you can sue based on fraud or malfeasance.

---

12 http://www.independent.org/publications/article.asp?id=1510
13 https://www.wbur.org/hereandnow/2018/04/09/hair-braiding-licenses

Government force comes in all shapes and sizes. Some force comes in the color of Blue. By trying to control the behavior of its citizens, law is used to justify all kinds of actions.

Current debate about the appropriate use of force when fighting non-violent crime is a good illustration. When 4 police officers can physically take down, with batons and Tasers, someone for selling individual cigarettes then something is out of whack. Yet, when we give government permission to have such a deep impact in our daily lives it doesn't matter if that permission was tacit or explicit.

At some point we must step back and examine whether we should be allowing government force, violence by any other measure, to regulate activities with no victims. This kind of 'victimless crime' *creates* victims in those who get caught up in the violence government leaves in its wake.

A popular meme embossed over the picture of a police officer reads 'Drugs can ruin your life… so, I'm going to arrest you, throw you in jail and ruin your life.' Granting leave to the State to use violence in controlling non-violent crime may be the biggest travesty we've allowed to happen.

Social Collision

The religion-based framework that the political right wishes to impose on the country stands in stark contrast to the moral hazard risk of the left's social welfare and protectionist policies.

On the right, the social, political commentary is largely autocratic.

- You may only marry if you follow our definition of marriage
- You may only do business if you follow my licensing schemes
- You may only get preferential tax treatment if you follow the rules that I like

On the left, the social, political commentary is *also* largely autocratic.

- You may not apply your personal views to any couple that wants to marry
- You many only do business if you follow my licensing schemes
- You may only get preferential tax treatment if you follow the rules that I like

A Practical Libertarian

The details behind the statements change, but the statements really do not. The right's licensing schemes tend to protect business and the left's tend to protect populations. The same with tax treatment. This is how things come out in practice, despite the right claiming they like small government and the left social freedoms.

When thinking of how the Right's licensing schemes are business centric think of the cosmetology license that protects the business owner who is currently licensed. Or, think of real estate licensing schemes where only licensed agents can sell a house. These businesses use their clout and the money that comes with establishment to convince legislators to pass laws restricting competition. The law of the market says that with restricted availability comes higher prices. And a black market. In this case a black market of underground hair braiders, and when there's a problem the customer has no recourse because they'd have to admit to illegal activity.

> *"Too many of these boards and commissions exist to stop competition, to stifle and protect the status quo. And we're changing that in Arizona."*
> AZ Governor Ducey

When thinking of how the Left's licensing schemes are population centric think rent control or stabilization. In order to lease property that you own, or get permits to build properties that you own, you must commit to rent at government set rates with limited ability to raise rents and recoup upgrade costs. This is distortionary in so many ways: It artificially raises rates for everyone other than those lucky enough to get the rent-controlled units. Costs are costs and owners must recover them to make a profit. After all, why else would they be in business if not to make a profit?

Rent control creates an adversarial condition between renters and landlords. Keeping some rent below market rates disincentivizes property owners from maintaining the property. The law of the market says that with restricted availability comes higher prices. And, a black market. In this case the black market becomes a bribery scheme to buy your way into a rent-controlled apartment. And again, you can't go to the authorities when there's a problem because you'd be admitting to illegal behavior.

In fact, in looking at the rent control issue, the Left's insistence on its virtues are so opposed to economic theory and research, that even far left economist Paul

Krugman ended a New York Times article on the dangers of rent control with "So now you know why economists are useless: when they actually do understand something, people don't want to hear about it."[14]

The Washington Post remarked, "Declining housing stock is just one of the many potential costs of rent controls; others include a deteriorating housing stock as landlords stop investing in their properties, and higher rents. Yes, higher, because rent control creates a two-tier housing market. There are cheap, price-stabilized apartments that rarely turn over, because why would you give up such a great deal? Then there are the uncontrolled apartments, which everyone else in the city has to fight over, bidding up the price."[15]

We can see these as demonstrations that it's generally thought that the right is more business centric and the left population centric. In practice it is more like the right protects the rights of those who take risk in starting and managing businesses, and the left those who are employed.

In a report authored in 2015 by the Obama White House Council on Economic Advisors and the Dept of Labor it was said "By one estimate, licensing restrictions cost millions of jobs nationwide and raise consumer expenses by over one hundred billion dollars."

In summarizing that report, Reason wrote "Yet stringent occupational licensing seldom delivers improved services or safety to consumers. In 10 out of the 12 empirical studies reviewed by the report authors, stricter licensing was not associated with quality improvements."[16]

The bigger question is begged, then. If each group wants to use licensing and tax schemes to their own benefit, differently, why are we using licensing and tax schemes for anyone's benefit? If it's not good for the goose it shouldn't be used by the gander.

The libertarian perspective on these is a little different. On marriage, the question they'd pose is: why is the government involved at all? It's a relatively new construct that with examination doesn't make much sense. "I love you so much, my Darling, that I want the government to get involved," said no one, ever.

---

14 https://www.nytimes.com/2000/06/07/opinion/reckonings-a-rent-affair.html
15 https://www.washingtonpost.com/opinions/2019/06/15/comeback-rent-control-just-time-make-housing-shortages-worse
16 https://reason.com/2015/07/31/white-house-occupational-licenses-report

A Practical Libertarian

Marriage started as a religious ceremony. It has morphed into a social contract that is often used by government for its own perpetuation. The government first started recognizing marriage in law alongside the Revenue Act of 1913 which imposed the income tax, shortly after the passage of the 16th amendment making such a tax legal. It wasn't until 1929 that all states had laws regarding the issuance of marriage licenses.

These registrations, marriage licenses, allowed the government to use the tax code to encourage the behaviors the party in power liked. Get a tax deduction for having children. Get a tax deduction for buying a house. Get a tax deduction for using the government defined and controlled retirement accounts (401k) instead of your own savings or brokerage accounts. The common theme is 'do what we want and we'll reward you'.

Marriage by itself serves two purposes that don't need government intervention. A religious recognition of a relationship, however your religion chooses to define that. And, estate planning for the care of each other in the marriage and their children. Estate planning may mean medical decision-making privilege in the case of one party's poor health, or it may be who gets what as an inheritance.

In my mind, a Practical Libertarian, this is better left to a contract between individuals. Religions have blessed marriages on their own for millennia and don't need government intervention to continue to serve their members. If you don't practice a religion then you don't need this at all and you can create whatever kind of civil ceremony you wish.

If two (or three or four) people wish to form a contract with each other granting medical decision making and sharing an interest in a household then that's not much different than 4 lawyers forming a partnership and declaring common ownership (and liability) in a law practice. Canceling such a contract, a divorce, determines the dissolution of the common assets and responsibilities, just as I've seen with a law partnership breaking up, and is a matter for agreement or civil court.

Moral Hazard

By being selective in whom they protect, the legislation of the left and right creates great moral hazard. To me it is the most objectionable part of government. (The

Libertarians don't generally 'have legislation' due to their minority status and their minimalist government views)

Each side chooses who should have advantage, and in granting that advantage allows a population to "take advantage of a situation by taking risks that others will pay for."[17]

In talking about selectivity here, I don't wish to ascribe evil intent. I wholly believe that each side believes what they are doing is right. A website devoted to exposing fallacy, defines the 'righteousness fallacy' as "Assuming that just because a person's intentions are good, they have the truth or facts on their side."[18] This can be rephrased 'The road to hell is paved with good intentions.'

You could devote an entire book around this fallacy and government.

- The 'food pyramid' fiasco where the federal government proscribed nutritional labelling and school lunch makeups that turned out to feed to the obesity epidemic.
- Alcohol Prohibition's enactment. And removal, after the predictable black market laid siege to our cities.
- Bridges, tunnels and high-speed trains 'to nowhere'.

What's as bad as the initial bad result of the good intention, is the downward spiral that it starts.

One 'hell' that we've paved our way to includes a drug black market that supports gangs and terrorist organizations around the world. We learned in the 1920's that a prohibition does not stop the behavior that it is designed to stop. It just pushes it underground.

Just like in the 1920's, we see illegal production around the world. That production is promulgated and protected by gangs and terrorists. The gangs kill each other to gain market share, and take a terrible human toll in moving the drugs to where they need to be sold. Locally, dealers become pawns and expendables in the greater scheme.

The government itself was responsible for hundreds of deaths during prohibition because they poisoned alcohol labeled for industrial use they knew would be

---

17 https://www.thebalance.com/moral-hazard-what-it-is-and-how-it-works-315515
18 https://www.logicallyfallacious.com/tools/lp/Bo/LogicalFallacies/239/Righteousness-Fallacy

redirected for consumption. Does a government that poisons its own people sound righteous to you, regardless the cause they were fighting?

In making the drugs illegal we've laid waste to whole populations. The people who use drugs fear getting treatment due to the threat of arrest. They end up getting arrested for crimes they commit to get money to pay the artificially inflated prices due to the black market. We've compromised whole countries in Central America and Southeast Asia where drug production is more profitable than food.

It's a vicious cycle.

Now, take the 'good intention' out of the equation.

- Legal drugs are kept out of the hands of children because gangs are no longer marketing to them, and they're behind the counter with alcohol that already has an age restriction and an infrastructure to support the security and enforcement.
- Drug gangs have lost their source of money, and with that went their power to corrupt and bribe their governments, or raise money for arms to protect their territory and product.
- South America and Southeast Asia starts producing benevolent crops to support their families and country without the danger of their Army, our CIA, or the US Military swooping in with helicopters to jail them. It becomes a safe, friendly place to visit on vacation.
- Casual users can do so safely because some street thug isn't watering down their product with stuff they don't understand like fentanyl. Potency is understood at the sales counter.
- Those with addictions can safely seek help without fear of arrest, and while they're being treated and still using, the product they're using follows a standard dose and is unlikely to kill them.

It may sound like an oversimplification, but it's not far-fetched.

It's an immutable fact that prohibition doesn't work. There will always be people who find drugs attractive for recreational use and who are willing to take the risk to find sellers. There will always be addicts who turn to crime to support their habits. You can be sure that there are people willing to risk their lives to produce and sell it illicitly because the black-market rewards are huge.

The question is, what is the cost to society if we discourage but allow the behavior compared to fighting it? Fighting it hasn't worked.

During his 2016 presidential campaign, Gary Johnson (L) was asked about heroin legalization by a mother who lost her child to a heroin overdose. His response was that her child had 'succumbed to prohibition'. Heroin in and by itself is addictive but not typically dangerous in the short term. Just look at the huge military population that used and got off it in, and returning from, Viet Nam.

Prohibition changes the equation. Johnson continued, "your supplier has now been arrested and put into jail, and now comes a new supplier of heroin, and the new supply of heroin. Visually you're taking the same dose that you've taken before, but it's of a different quality and a different quantity, and it ends up killing you."[19]

Now, again, don't get lost in the extremes of the argument. Addiction is a terrible thing, but where there is a vacuum, an underground market will always spring up. And rarely are the benefits of the vacuum better than the unintended consequences.

It can be debated in many neighborhoods whether the gangs are a bigger consequence, or the threats of violence from law enforcement. People injured, killed, and property damaged in 'No Knock Raids' for non-violent crimes is a crime itself. It doesn't take a swat team to arrest someone for possessing small quantities of marijuana, but we read about such activities all the time.

Moral hazard comes from both sides of the political spectrum.

- Highly subsidized flood insurance allows people to build in flood prone areas and the taxpayer catches the tab
- No cost healthcare allows people to avoid health improving habits
- High value welfare keeps people from working and being self sufficient
- Corporations get away with insufficient compliance and bad behavior because there's a lack of direct accountability in the C-suite. Think of AIG and Lehman in 2008. How many people were prosecuted? (I'll give you a hint, it's none.)[20]

---

19 http://cnnpressroom.blogs.cnn.com/2016/06/22/transcript-cnn-libertarian-town-hall-moderated-by-chris-cuomo/
20 https://www.washingtonpost.com/news/wonk/wp/2013/09/12/this-is-a-complete-list-of-wall-street-ceos-prosecuted-for-their-role-in-the-financial-crisis/?noredirect=on&utm_term=.80d461593336

'Entangling Alliances'

Under both parties, we've been in a condition of permanent war.

In George Washington's farewell speech, he warned about the dangers of 'permanent alliances'. Jefferson's inaugural address just one term later similarly spoke of, "Peace, commerce, and honest friendship with all nations - entangling alliances with none."

How did we get to non-stop war? Congress started a long tradition of shirking its duties. According to the Constitution, only congress has the power to declare war.

The cold war, post WWII, allowed a hyper-militarization and led to an undeclared proxy war in Korea... and Eisenhauer's famous warning about the 'military industrial complex'.

Congress sat idly by and allowed Kennedy, Johnson, and then Nixon to fight in Viet Nam and Cambodia with neither real challenge nor a formalized declaration of war.

Back to the cold war with Reagan and then Bush I, ultimately helping break up the USSR. This had some positive effects like the reunification of Germany but caused many of the smaller republics decades of hardship, strife, and thousands of deaths because of the leadership vacuum it left behind.

Clinton fought the beginnings of al-Qaeda, and I remember that time for his bombing of an aspirin factory on unverified information. With close timing to the movie Wag the Dog, the action was rumored to have been intended to cover the breaking Monica Lewinsky story.

Bush II took the al-Qaeda fight further after 9/11 and we've had troops dying in the Middle East ever since. And, an increase in domestic surveillance and domestic militarization to go with it.

In the course of this time line we've chosen to remove leaders of other countries, trying to deploy democracy like it was a universal truth. Our nation building efforts have been largely unsuccessful and we spend our lives and fortunes carelessly.

Alarmingly, we set our alliances carelessly too. The 'enemy of my enemy' does not automatically make someone my friend. Tight alliances with Saudi Arabia because they oppose Iran ignores the terrible human rights record they hold. It's great that they're now allowing women to drive, but this one allowance does not make up for their treatment of women, their minorities, and their LGBT communities in general. Their practices are abhorrent and we should not lend them credence by our alliance.

Sadly, this is not the only example. Partnering with Central and South American countries because they oppose Venezuela, or because they let our military in to terrorize their citizens while fighting the drug war puts us in bad company. It poses moral issues when we have to turn our heads and ignore bad behaviors to keep our alliances strong.

I believe that the history of a people determines what form of government will work for them. In the United States we have done well with a republic, shortcomings discussed here notwithstanding, because our history of independence goes back well before our founding.

It was in a search for this freedom that the first settlers came. This cannot be said of most other places in the world. It is only our hubris that allows us to meddle in other people's affairs thinking we can do it for them – create a government in OUR image that they can figure out how to operate. Other peoples tolerate a government that their history has let them learn to accept. If they choose to accept or overthrow that system it is on them to do it. Without their population's support and knowledge, it falls apart quickly as we have seen in many of the countries we have invaded.

Entangling alliances also affect markets.

Markets

So called 'free trade' agreements aren't so free. NAFTA prompted a net migration of jobs to lower labor cost Mexico, while we sent them subsidized farm products their own farmers couldn't compete with.

> "It is easy to see why someone who might in general support free trade would oppose NAFTA. The winners are the businesses that are in a position to take advantage of access to cheap labor in Mexico. The losers are the manufacturing

> *workers in the United States who will now have to accept lower wages or lose their job."*[21]

You'd think a 'free' policy would be one page. 'We would like to trade freely with you, you agree to trade freely with us.' No, these agreements are thousands of pages of exceptions, rules, and "if-then" statements about trade that have very little to do with trade.[22] It is often about protectionism and negotiating to protect our best markets while trying to exploit theirs.

The obverse of free trade is embargo. We have many embargoes. None of them work. We've never embargoed a country into submission. We have helped impoverish the peoples of Cuba, North Korea, the former Soviet eastern bloc. We foster hate, derision and jealousy when we embargo countries. This feeds back into a self-reinforcing loop where the local governments then blame us for their problems, the people protest and reinforce the government for hating on us.

Most embargoes aren't unanimous among the world's governments and so are ineffective. In the most onerous cases, like Iran and North Korea, the dictators are able to insulate themselves from the ill effects and those that pay the worst price are the populace.

Market Protection

Market protection extends beyond trade. We protect and regulate products and markets internally too. Just ask about the global price of sugar and then look at what we pay in the US. The US protects sugar manufacturers from foreign, *and domestic*, competition and rewards them with regulated, high prices. Tariffs are imposed on imported sugar, so it doesn't take market share from our domestic producers. Sugar is a commodity, so pricing fluctuates, but Americans pay almost double world prices. This was probably a big reason that soft drink manufacturers moved to high fructose corn syrup.

What does this do to consumers? We all pay higher food bills because of this scheme, an estimated 1.5 billion dollars a year.

---

21 http://cepr.net/blogs/beat-the-press/nafta-and-free-trade-do-not-belong-in-the-same-sentence
22 NAFTA is 2000 pages, TPP over 5000.

There is a raisin cartel. It is called the US Federal Government (formally the *Raisin Administrative Committee*), and if you grow too many raisins (or sour cherries, or dozens of other products) they will confiscate them or require they be destroyed.[23]

This is part of the Agricultural Adjustment Act of 1938 (cherries were added later) and covers dozens of products other than raisins including rye, prunes, pecans, barley, and wool in a central planning scheme with control boards determining what gets sold and what gets kept off the market.

When someone says we're a capitalist country, it's ok to say 'only somewhat'. These 'internal' trade schemes, like the perennial 'Farm Bill', do all of the bad things we've talked about thus far: they perpetuate the fallacy of good intentions, they distort the capitalist market which is the most efficient way of regulating the production and sale of goods and services, and they create a huge moral hazard by taking the risk out of an activity that should be self-limiting.

Regulation of Everything

We long ago reached a point where there are so many regulations and laws that no one could possibly understand or know them all. In 2017 the code of Federal Regulations was 186,374 pages.[24] That's just the federal regulations. Now add in state, local and county laws, zoning, and other restrictions on your actions and person and it can't be called anything other than repressive.

Google 'ridiculous laws' and you'll come up with a never-ending supply of joke worthy items like: it is illegal to color thousand island dressing a color that isn't customary for thousand island dressing. It is illegal to include the word 'zombie' in the name of a wine. "7 USC §2623(d) makes it a federal crime for a USDA employee to reveal how a potato producer voted in a potato referendum."[25]

The worst outcome of this is what I call the 'habit of fraud'.

- The speed limit is 65 but everyone goes 80. It's ok, everyone else is doing it and I'm a good driver.

---

23 https://www.sovereignman.com/trends/no-i-am-not-joking-the-us-government-centrally-plans-raisin-production-16911/
24 https://www.federalregister.gov/uploads/2018/03/cfrTotalPages2017.pdf
25 https://twitter.com/CrimeADay/status/1111424530528915458

- The income tax form says only certain things are deductible, people inflate the numbers to increase their refund. It's ok, everyone else is doing it and I really need the extra refund for my kids.
- The local building code says only a licensed plumber can replace a water heater, but the homeowner does it him or herself.

All of these little things build habit in our minds that it's ok to bend the rules. Who even knows all the rules we're bending?

There are so many ways that we may or may not be in violation of the innumerable codes and laws that we stop caring. The creep from something really minor like inflating a charity donation on our tax return to something major, like embezzlement, happens all the time. There are people in the news all the time who are surprised that they got caught.

No one is Watching the Watchers

The United States government has become a behemoth surveillance machine sucking up data on your every move, every tweet, every phone call, every ping off of a cell phone tower. Your data may be aggregated with other people's to make broad assumptions, or it may be picked apart to identify you. Your political thoughts in posting to Facebook, your physical movements in cell tower records, your associations by who you email are all collected, analyzed and stored for future use by the federal government.

Recent Supreme Court decisions have helped to define some of these and started to reign in some of the practices, but they leave in place a whole host of tactics that clearly defy the founding documents.

In Riley v California in 2014, the Supreme Court found that search of a cell phone could not be done without a warrant. California had argued that the search was legal because, like searching the pockets of an arrestee for the protection of the officer or preservation of evidence, the cell phone was on Riley's person.

Chief Justice Roberts argued that "With all they contain, and all they may reveal, they hold for many Americans 'the privacies of life'. The fact that technology now allows an individual to carry such information in his hand does not make the information any less worthy of the protection for which the Founders fought."

In Carpenter v United States (2018), the Supreme Court rightfully determined that a warrant was needed to search phone records held by a cell provider. This case put limits on what is known as the '3rd party doctrine' which says that if you've given information to a third party you've effectively given up your right to privacy and the information is fair game without warrant.

The Carpenter case is interesting because Chief Justice Roberts sided with the 4 liberal judges on the court. Reigning in the 3rd party doctrine was important here. The 3rd party in this case was the phone company who keeps records as part of conducting their business. However, the communications between the phone and phone company are encrypted and the phone company includes a privacy statement in their contract, just like your bank, defining who has access to your data. This creates an expectation of privacy and the elevated requirements of 'probable cause' that goes with it.

The Bill of Rights is pretty clear on this matter. "The right of the people to be secure in their persons, houses, papers, and effects, against unreasonable searches and seizures, shall not be violated, and no warrants shall issue, but upon probable cause, supported by oath or affirmation, and particularly describing the place to be searched, and the persons or things to be seized."

Despite phone records recording your locations (at seemingly all times), we have a fundamental right of movement.

This 'right to travel', though not identified explicitly in the Constitution was listed in Article 4 of the Articles of Confederation. It has been understood to be a part of the 5th amendment granting equal protection under the law. It was recognized as a right as early as 1868 in Crandall v Nevada when Nevada was told they could not tax someone leaving the state.

Despite recent case law, the surveillance state has been well documented through groups like Wikileaks and investigations by Libertarian think tanks.

The Hill website wrote just this past year about the CIA's surveillance state. "Over time, the CIA upper echelon has secretly developed all kinds of policy statements and legal rationales to justify routine, widespread surveillance on U.S. soil of citizens who aren't suspected of terrorism or being a spy."[26]

---

26 https://thehill.com/opinion/national-security/414804-surveillance-state-is-alive-well-and-operating-against-us-all

The ACLU writes about surveillance by the National Security Administration, saying that "The government's surveillance programs have infiltrated most of the communications technologies we have come to rely on. They are largely enabled by a problematic law passed by Congress — the FISA Amendments Act (FAA), which is set to expire this year — along with Executive Order 12,333, the primary authority invoked by the NSA to conduct surveillance outside of the United States."[27]

The government has used our fears against us to get us to be quiet about such activities. They're only reading emails of foreigners who are conspiring against us! They're only stopping bad guys! Who can argue with that? Except it's not true.

Because these things are mired in secrecy, and behind a veil of 'National Security', they can't possibly be addressed by the People as they oversee Congress to make informed election decisions.

The Pandering Drive to Socialism

> "When the people find that they can vote themselves money, that will herald the end of the republic." Benjamin Franklin

Free College, Universal Medicare, is there nothing that the government can't make better by providing it for free?

Except nothing is free. Remember above? "The government has nothing that it doesn't take from the people by force." The left's drive to socialism is a divisive use of class warfare to enrage those who feel left out of the American Dream. If you grew up poor and struggle to get by it sure sounds good. The government is taking from someone else. Almost like Robin Hood.

We've set up a tax system that is *SO* progressive that the lower 50% of taxpayers only pay 3 percent of the taxes and an average rate of 3.75%.[28] This likely means that the vast majority of those in the bottom 50% pay no taxes at all. The income cut-off was a little over $40,000 per return.

---

27 https://www.aclu.org/issues/national-security/privacy-and-surveillance/nsa-surveillance
28 https://taxfoundation.org/summary-latest-federal-income-tax-data-2018-update/

A Practical Libertarian

Half the people don't have incentive for their elected officials to be careful with the people's money because they're not paying in. They have no skin in the game! Free healthcare, free college? Count me in. Rent control? Yes siree!

In fact, it's even worse than that. The Earned Income Credit average payout is now almost $2500 and that went to 27 million households.[29] We're rewarding people for not improving themselves.

The drive to socialism as seen in the popularity of Bernie Sanders and Alexandria Ocasio-Cortez panders to those who have nothing to lose. That's so insidious because of the culture it creates. Why would you want to do better financially if it means becoming one of 'them'... Let's not disincentivize success!

It's insidious because of the duopoly it creates. Bernie can talk all day about how he feels the pain of the working class, but he gets to choose between several houses to go home to at night. Hardly the experience anyone but the 1% get to have, and the contrast is lost on the masses.

Even Alexandria Ocasio-Cortez has been lured into the fray choosing to represent her working-class constituency while wearing thousand-dollar skirts. Not even sworn in yet and she had already adopted the 'do as I say, not as I do' philosophy that so many 'poverty fighters' seem to have.

We have many examples of socialism's ill effects. Just look at Venezuela. In 1991 it was in the top 3 richest countries in the Americas. From the election of its first socialist leader you can track a very straight line to where they are now. In ruin economically and socially. Very much a civil war with people starving.

Socialism expects that government control can anticipate the needs of its people better than a free market.

In 2015 Bernie Sanders said "You don't necessarily need a choice of 23 underarm spray deodorants or of 18 different pairs of sneakers when children are hungry in this country." This is really a false dichotomy to imply that if we had less choice in scents and strengths, that we would be feeding more children.

In fact, there are choices because people buy them. If Johnson and Johnson isn't selling a particular scent, or Converse isn't selling a particular style of shoe they stop making it and put their efforts where they will be rewarded.

---

29 https://usafacts.org/search?query=earned%20income%20credit, 2016 numbers, the latest available

Government controlled enterprises cannot respond to consumer sentiment in the same way. I can easily see a scenario where a company that manufactures an unpopular scent gets the government to continue manufacturing the bad product because it has a lot of lobbyists.

Don't we hear about similar stories in the news with unnecessary military bases that can't be closed because of some congressman's constituency? Or "Language inserted into the federal budget over the objection of the Obama administration by Senator Thad Cochran, Republican of Mississippi, directed the Coast Guard to build a $640 million National Security Cutter in Mississippi that the Coast Guard says it does not need."[30] Or Senator Collins in Maine who managed to get a billion dollar ship built at the Bath Iron Works that the military didn't ask for, just because it brought jobs to her state.

Private enterprise advances by testing appetites for new products, and financial backers invest capital in their ability to deliver. An interesting article by John Tamny discussed Presidential Candidate Elizabeth Warren's response to all questions with "I have a plan for that." It seems there is nothing she isn't willing to exert Government force to fix.

The article speaks about how the children's cartoon Peppa Pig would not exist in a socialist country because government would never have anticipated the need. "You see, no one was demanding Peppa before 2004, and no politician was promising this most entertaining of cartoon series. The lack of demand didn't matter. In the profit-motivated world, creative individuals backed by intrepid investors are constantly coming up with new ideas to remove unease from our lives, make us more efficient, improve our health, and in the case of Peppa, entertain us."[31]

Tamny concludes "What could Warren offer us other than the inefficient delivery of what already exists?"

In many ways this is the *democracy* that the founders warned us about... two wolves and a sheep voting on what to have for dinner: A growing majority of the country that pays little or no taxes deciding how to tax everyone else.

---

30 https://www.nytimes.com/2015/12/21/us/politics/hospitality-and-gambling-interests-delay-closing-of-dollar1-billion-tax-loophole.html
31 https://www.realclearmarkets.com/articles/2019/05/31/peppa_pig_mocks_the_insulting_conceit_of_elizabeth_warren_103757.html

Spending

What happens when the party in power gets what they want, and the party in power changes every 4 to 8 years? Everyone gets what they want! The priorities are schizophrenic, and spending is runaway.

At the time of writing, Summer 2019, we are looking at record breaking deficits and a debt that doesn't seem real at over a full year's GDP[32]. This is from a Republican President and, until recently, a Republican majority congress. The party that should be fiscally conservative. Do as I say, not as I do… we've heard that before, no?

The left's race to socialism only bodes worse for deficit hawks who know that this can only persist so long before the piper has to be paid.

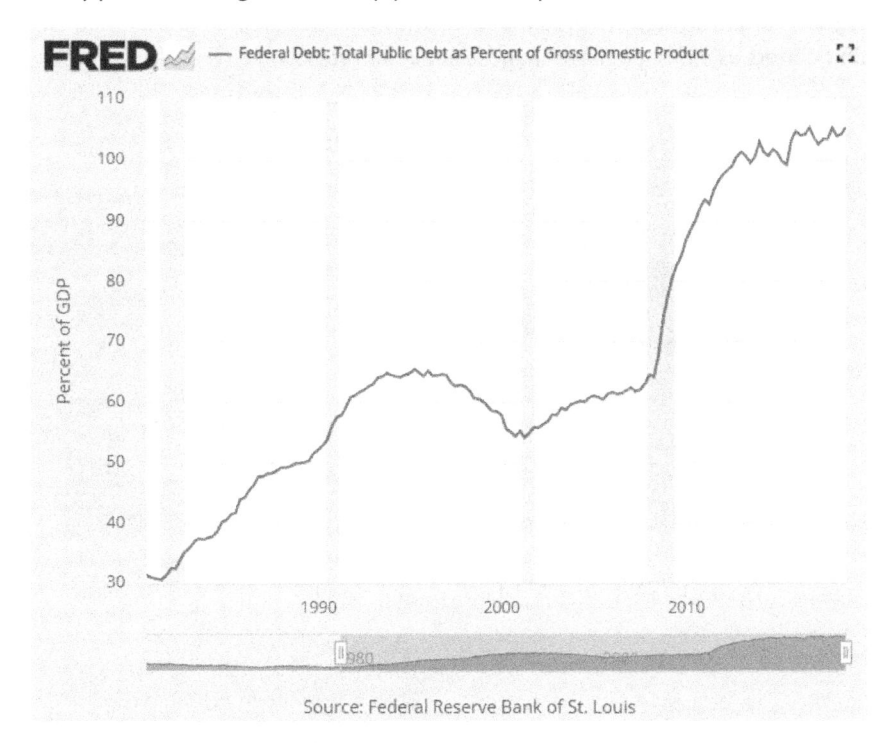

Source: Federal Reserve Bank of St. Louis

Cutting spending is inevitable because the debt will become crushing. At some point. Economists can't agree on what the level is where things tank, and that's why waiting till it's too late is so frightening. It could be 1.2x GDP, it could be 1.5x.

---

32 https://fred.stlouisfed.org/series/GFDEGDQ188S

Do we wait till we're crushed to find out or can we agree that the debt is so huge and looming that it needs to be addressed TODAY?

We're getting away with debt now because of the very low interest rates. When they revert to average, we won't be able to keep up.

Because interest rates are so low right now the Treasury Department has been front loading maturity dates. This is great in the short term because low rates save us money. But if the Federal Reserve ever loses hold on rates, the effect on the annual budget will be almost immediate as over 60% of the debt will need to be reissued within 5 years.

This is terrifying! In 2020 the estimate has debt service (interest) at 10% of the budget. If interest rates increase modestly that will have an immediate drain on the public coffers as all that debt refinances at higher rates.

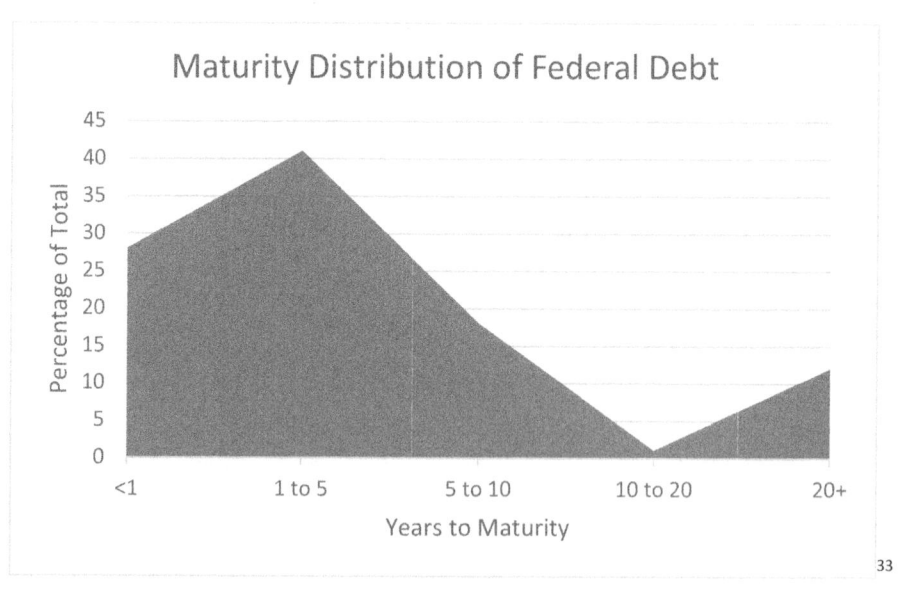

Maturity Distribution of Federal Debt

[33]

---

[33] https://www.quandl.com/data/USTREASURY/MATDIS-Maturity-Distribution-and-Average-Length-of-Marketable-Interest-Bearing-Public-Debt

Rights and Responsibilities

Let's talk for a moment about rights and responsibilities. We have the US Bill of Rights to start with and while it does not enumerate all our rights, it does a pretty good job.

The Bill of Rights covers freedoms and liberties that we have, and declares that they are endowed to us by our creator, whomever we believe that to be.

What exactly are rights? Dictionary.com defines a Right (Noun) as "a moral or legal entitlement to have or obtain something or to act in a certain way" and a Human Right as "a right that is believed to belong justifiably to every person."

Rights in this sense (and in the Bill of Rights) are all things that are free to us. The right to a fair trial, the right to be free from search, the right to a free press. We expect the government to respect those, but no one is put out for us to get them. Our use of one right doesn't affect anyone else's ability to use theirs.

Democratic party factions volleying for power right now would like to expand this definition to include things OWED from others. As example, candidates, and the United Nations, have declared health care a human right.

In order to have health care we need several things, it's not something like a liberty that comes out of thin air. At a minimum, we need knowledge, supplies and labor. Hopefully the labor has the knowledge long enough to practice it into skill!

In the modern age of the internet we can make the knowledge freely available with books online and YouTube videos. But, can we have a right to someone else's labor? If not their labor directly, then the money to pay for someone else's labor and supplies? (which arguably comes from yet another person's labor, the taxpayers).

We ought to be extremely cautious about calling things rights that depend on the labor of others. Boiled down it sounds like slavery. You must give up your work, your labor, your hard-earned treasure to pay for the 'rights' of others.

We can and should talk about a safety net. We can and should talk about taking care of the vulnerable in our society – people with mental and physical disabilities. But when we declare that people have an inherent right to the labor of others, we've given the phrase, human right, a new definition and new scope.

Paired with the Bill of Rights, there should also be a bill of responsibilities. We have the responsibility to not harm others. We have the responsibility to take care that our actions don't infringe on the rights of others.

When we create rights out of other people's labor, we make our actions subject to scrutiny. If I have a human right to healthcare and it's paid for by the public, then does the public have the right to control what I ingest under the guise of keeping me healthy? After all, the public is paying for my care, they should be able to force me to be healthier! And the corollary of that is, if I'm stupid and eat an all sugar diet, you can't refuse to cover the resulting illnesses because it's a human right.

This is a scary line we cross. If we must give up liberties, other rights, to get those with dependencies, then I contend those aren't rights at all.

Symptoms Summarized

These are all symptoms of a broken system. We've reached several thresholds all at once.

- The extremist sides are dividing us to artificially inflate their cases and create animus and hate between us.
- They use the force of government to threaten us into choosing sides, further shoring up their power.
- They use social division and rules around the divisions to create battle lines.
- They create foreign alliances to both distract from domestic ills and perpetuate a military globalism.
- They spy on us under the guise of national security.
- They've spent us into oblivion with no visible way out. The debt discussed above is the official tally and does not include debt issued by federal agencies, owed to the social security trust fund, owed by states and local governments, or underfunded pension obligations.
- Proposed rights that violate other rights.

Will it take a catastrophe to get people to stop yelling at each other and start listening?

Libertarians and Factions

Hopefully we can agree that the current system is pretty broken. We may believe this for different reasons, and that's ok. We have a starting point: Agreement that *something* has to change.

Many of you probably read the title and thought the Libertarians were some wacky anarchist group who have never been able to field a viable candidate. You may be right.

The Libertarian Party is similar to the Republicans and Democrats in that there's a wide range of thought from centrist like mine to anarchists that don't believe in much if any government. The Democrats vary from 'blue dog' to socialist, and the Republicans from 'log cabin' or Rockefeller to neoconservative. Some are 'big tent' believers, some are somewhat more singularly focused.

Because Libertarians, by nature, tend to be individualistic, they're difficult to corral into coordinated action.

See the conflict here? Politics requires much coordinated action and Libertarians don't believe in coordinating!

The biggest obstacle to Libertarian elected officials is that most Libertarians don't believe there should be so many elected officials. Another obstacle to electing Libertarians is getting enough to agree on coming out to vote.

Working with the Libertarian Party of Florida, we used to say trying to get Libertarians together was like herding cats. In a state of 21 million we had trouble getting 100 Libertarians to an Annual Convention. This despite polls showing common ideals with 50% or more of the people, and 27 percent of the registered voters having no party affiliation.

Some of this is the branding of the Republican and Democrat parties using their politics of division to make people think they have to identify as such. They are both quick to say that voting Libertarian is a 'wasted vote'.

Some of this is lack of consistent branding by Libertarians and failure to gain enough consensus internally. After all, if you can't present a unified front, you look like a loose collection of activists instead of a results-oriented team.

A Practical Libertarian

Meetings of Libertarians commonly consist of discussions about libertarianism and who is the 'better' or 'more pure' Libertarian. The divisions in the party are more concerned with getting their spin on things in the platform than getting the general ideas out to the public.

Friends in the Party openly discussed voting Republican or Democrat in the 2008 campaign *against* Bob Barr, the Libertarian Candidate. Why? He wasn't libertarian enough. Barr had roots in the Republican party and though he had campaigned against runaway government he couldn't pull in the social liberal side of the party.

Gary Johnson in 2012 and 2016's presidential election highlighted another faction: those that believe that recreational drug legalization is the number one issue. Despite conquering the monumental task of gaining ballot access in all 50 states, Johnson's marijuana use was a distraction from a national campaign and did not help the Libertarian's desire to be taken seriously on a national stage.

Johnson's track record in his home state of New Mexico was stellar. Two term governor, term-limited out of office. He left with very high poll ratings, a budget surplus and everyone was happy. But, somewhere along the line he became the face of a stoner movement and the butt of jokes on the late-night circuit. "What is Aleppo?" Johnson asked during one interview.

The Republican Liberty Caucus is a libertarian leaning group trying to bring about change from inside the Republican party. It's banner holder, Ron Paul, and son Rand, espouse liberty minded policies, but in a party dominated by the further right, they remain just another fringe movement. And, although they get occasional headlines it's just as likely they're being chided by colleagues for stalling a bill rather than heard for their substance.

There is perpetual debate among my Libertarian friends about whether to remain independent as a big L party, or work from within one of the other parties. Both have merit and problems.

Standing alone we haven't, historically, had a big tent mentality. Because of this, local and state parties are more like social clubs where people get together to discuss how libertarian they are and how upset they are with the system.

When working within the Republican and Democratic parties, the 'politics of division' crowd always speaks with a louder voice because to promote their parties they must foment anger and urgency.

Now, I'm not trying to denigrate Libertarians. I agree most closely with their tenets, but we have to take an honest and blunt look at what works and doesn't work in politics. If we're going to make a difference we have to be heard widely and loudly. Getting heard will require some changes.

Why 'Practical Libertarianism'

Can you name one thing the government does really well?

This was the question I thought about when deciding to take a stab at writing this book.

I have friends on both ends of the standard political spectrum, from green liberal, to very religious conservative. Both ends have lots of things they want government to do, but when asked to name something the government does well, neither side could name anything.

Government doesn't do national healthcare really well, neither in how we manage Medicare/Medicaid and the VA system nor how we regulate (and require) healthcare insurance. We haven't managed social security really well, considering retirees will soon see no return on the investment they paid in. It's going to be broke soon without drastic action that we can't find the intestinal fortitude to address.

We manage to be the policemen of the world at the cost of a broken budget at home. We nation build and end up permanently managing (and supporting) the countries where we've been, fighting the scourge of the leadership vacuums we created.

We don't manage welfare well. There are over 89 competing means-tested programs, and government has a bureaucratic cost much higher than most private charities. Having spent trillions of dollars in the Great Society experiment our poverty rate has changed little.

We don't manage education terribly well. Primary and secondary schools have terribly uneven and unequal outcomes based on where you happen to have been born. And, the government subsidy of college student loans has allowed costs to consistently rise well above the rate of inflation by distorting the free market.

We haven't had our freedoms protected well; they've been eroding for decades. Government interference in every aspect of our lives has increased along with the danger that government intervention will bankrupt or kill us.

Our transportation networks have been neglected. The interstate system started during President Eisenhower's administration was quite a marvel, but funding has been raided and maintenance ignored.

The FDA does a good job at protecting the health of the citizens, but at a very high cost in unintended consequences and bureaucratic overhead. Competition and fuzzy lines between the FDA and the Department of Agriculture cause issues territorially and with conflicting standards and regulations. Regulation and lack of competition artificially raise prices for medications, and don't get me started on how hospitals and practitioners set prices…

So how, then, can we look at this track record of mediocrity (at best) and think *more* government is the answer to anything?

A Problem with Scale

The opposite of more government is less. The true libertarianism of rugged individuals sounds great to many of us, and on a frontier it made a lot of sense. You wanted to protect your rights, protect yourself from invaders and the intrusion of people with authoritarian ideals.

But I contend this doesn't work at scale. For one reason.

Some people are assholes.

There, I said it. (Usually I try and keep that to my 'inner voice')

Strict libertarianism requires the participation of everyone to take care of themselves. It requires that everyone understand where the boundaries of their actions need to be to protect the rights of the people next to them and that just doesn't happen.

People drive drunk. People violate your property rights by throwing trash out their car windows and dumping into ditches on the side of the road. If you have property on a hill, someone below you will build high and block your view. If you live on water someone upstream will pollute it.

Restaurant owners, drug manufacturers, and slaughterhouses neglect cleanliness standards. Examples of all of these can be found easily enough in the news daily, or with a quick google search. I won't call any out here specifically because these stories are so ubiquitous.

There are free market, private alternatives to government for many of the tasks government performs, but, like the discussion on current commitments that follows, these will take time to develop and implement and won't be an instant fix even if we could swing public opinion in an instant.

Not everyone understands or respects the concept of personal responsibility so we must *work together* to protect our rights. This is the difference between a pure libertarian and a 'Practical Libertarian' viewpoint.

Rules to help us live together aren't all bad. Rules to set standards in safety and building can be beneficial... *as long as they don't prevent self-sufficiency.*

In an article for the Foundation for Economic Education (FEE), Tabitha Alloway neatly summarizes Bastiat's *The Law:* 'Justice is the use of collective force (law) to secure persons, liberty, and property, maintaining each in its right' and the perversion of law as 'any use of force for reasons beyond the purposes of securing persons, liberty, and property.'[34]

There is legitimate use for law well beyond what the 'pure' Libertarians believe in. But, not nearly as much as we have today. We've listed all kinds of actions that show perversion of the law: beyond the purposes of securing persons, liberty and property.

Personally, I get less libertarian the closer I get to home. There's really very little I want of the federal government. Protect me from invaders, foreign and domestic. Set up a system of justice so I can get relief from fraud, violence and damaging products. And get out of the way of the markets so that good products and services win over bad and they aren't chosen by a corrupt or misguided regulator.

Closer to home, I'm happy to have the roads paved uniformly by my town and highways by my state. This is a common Libertarian theme, 'who will build the roads?' when discounting the role of government. I also like that the flowers in the

---

34 https://fee.org/articles/french-protesters-learn-bastiat-was-right-about-the-law

town square are sponsored and paid for by a private company in exchange for space for a small plaque with their name.

Current Commitments

In thinking about transitioning to a more libertarian government and way of life, one of the mistakes the Libertarian Party makes is presenting new scenarios in a vacuum. We won't get elected and entrusted with Government with the more extreme political ideals. It will take cross-party cooperation to gain majority numbers. Transitioning will also take time to phase in new programs.

For example, we have had Social Security almost 85 years, since it was signed into law in 1935 by President Roosevelt. People have been conditioned over their lifetimes to expect the payout for what they've paid in. Their lifetime of planning followed this model. Those of us of a certain age cannot just abandon what we put in and lose any benefit from it.

Yes, it's a Ponzi scheme, and we could and should be doing better, but we can't just end it tomorrow. There must be a transition to what comes next. That can take different forms but given its ubiquity in every resident's lives, it's likely to be a very long crossover period.

Even if you could imagine paying out lump sums to everyone that paid in and ending the Social Security Administration immediately, there aren't enough investments to put all that money into in a short period of time. Dumping that much cash into the economic system in such a short period would cause unimaginable bubbles that will have people running back for protection in little time at all.

The bureaucratic behemoths of crop subsidies and flood insurance will take half a decade to unwind without being fatally disruptive. The markets will adapt but must be given time to find their center before the rug is pulled out on current custom.

Morphing out of some of these big government programs will require some finesse as they've become part of the bedrock of our daily lives. Literally, the bedrock of people's lives – their homes. Flood insurance modifications, especially, will have ripple effects.

In 2017 the Wall St Journal wrote about a house that had been flooded and repaired 22 times to the tune of 1.8 million dollars (for a $600,000 house).[35] Why has this responsibility fallen on the people? Because we've allowed the moral hazard of someone thinking they can live where they want and someone else will pay when their bad decision comes to fruition.

Moral hazard isn't hard to find; this is just one example. It's also a demonstration of why it will be hard to unwind because people have invested in their homes in thousands of flood plains across the country. This will hurt some people. (Yes, perhaps righteously since they DID build or buy a house in a flood plain, but none-the-less...) There have been commitments made that we can't break or modify lightly.

Federal Taxation

With a debt that is greater than a year's GDP we can't just eliminate the level of income that comes from our current income taxes. We can work to replace it with something less onerous, something that doesn't require government interference and intrusion into our daily activities.

Among Libertarians there is much discussion about taxation. Memes saying 'taxation is theft' abound, yet there are some problems we agree are common. The one thing we all agree on, when discussing taxation, is that the IRS and income tax are oppressive and should be abolished.

Income taxes hurt us in many ways. The first is the deep intrusion of the government into our daily lives that it fosters.

The IRS demands to know the source of our income so it can be taxed. It demands to know how we choose to spend our money because some of our spending is allowed to be deductible.

The second is how much energy and money is spent trying to accommodate a tax code that has grown so large that no one, not even tax specialists, actually know what is taxable and what is not. A few years ago, a tax preparer organization had a

---

35 https://www.wsj.com/articles/one-house-22-floods-repeated-claims-drain-federal-insurance-program-1505467830

competition where a group of experts were given the same details for a return. No two returns came out the same. A tax code that can't be understood needs to go.

TaxFoundation.Org has calculated that over 8.9 billion (yes, with a 'b') hours were spent in 2016 complying with IRS requirements and this costs the economy $409 billion.[36] Imagine if people could turn that back into their households and businesses back into their products!

The third is how easily the tax code is manipulated to reward or punish as those in power desire. Just looking at its complexity and length, it has been weaponized. It is beyond fixing.

Majority Numbers are Needed to Win Elections

Clearly, the idea of politics is to enact your desired policies and having libertarian ideals is no different. Despite historical difficulty finding ways to work cooperatively, it is imperative that we do so to further the goals of libertarianism and put a stop to the divisive, rights incursion that the major parties have perpetuated.

Getting together to discuss politics and utopian worlds is great fun, but if we really want to affect change then we must change our ways to enable that to happen.

Libertarians are the party that champions the freedoms and rights embodied in our constitution. It is incumbent on us to work with different viewpoints to find areas we can agree on and start moving policy in a freer direction.

Where Can We Compromise and Where Can't We?

The hard north Libertarians (if Republicans and Democrats are right and left, let's use north for Libertarians as in my diagram in the early pages) will tell you that "Libertarian thought emphasizes the dignity of each individual, which entails both rights and responsibility [...] Because individuals are moral agents, they have a right to be secure in their life, liberty, and property."[37]

---

36 https://taxfoundation.org/compliance-costs-irs-regulations/
37 https://www.cato.org/commentary/key-concepts-libertarianism

This doesn't mean there aren't disagreements about those rights with other parties, and even within. Subjects like abortion and gun control set people at odds even in a party that believes in individual rights.

The Libertarian platform plank on abortion reads "Recognizing that abortion is a sensitive issue and that people can hold good-faith views on all sides, we believe that government should be kept out of the matter, leaving the question to each person for their conscientious consideration."[38]

Abortion has been a dividing topic as long as it has existed. It is especially problematic in the Libertarian Party because it sets two ideals at odds.

Very often the libertarian ideals are described as 'life, liberty and property rights'. What is at odds is a religious view of 'life' and the libertarian 'liberty'. Some religions view life as beginning at conception without regard for whether the fertilized egg has implanted and actually become a pregnancy. We see this in some people's disagreement with embryo research, and contraceptives.

Some take the Bible more literally that life begins at birth with the first breath and read Genesis 2-7 "God formed man of the dust of the ground, and breathed into his nostrils the breath of life; and man became a living soul."

Others differentiate the scientific definition of 'life' (a distinct system of cells) and personhood. Personhood asks when an egg, embryo, or fetus becomes something independent of the pregnant woman's body.

Roe v Wade addressed that personhood question by setting it at viability, as when that developing child could live independently from its mother's physiological support. The 50/50 survival rate for premature birth happens between 24 and 25 weeks. That's towards the end of the 2nd trimester and about where Roe delineates lawful and unlawful abortion (subject to state law).

Given the close polling between pro-choice and anti-choice I believe the current platform plank is appropriate with the current restrictions of Roe. As Libertarians (big L) we must recognize the role that religious liberty plays in this. Constraints must be placed between one person's religious beliefs and another's liberty. As a matter of 'conscientious consideration', if you have religious views opposing

---

38 https://www.lp.org/platform/

abortions then don't get one. Allowing your religious views to constrict my rights opens yourself up to the same and that's where we draw the line.

Another contentious issue has no accepted boundaries yet. That is gun control.

Hard north Libertarians believe in the 2nd amendment with no restrictions. It is a right explicitly declared in our founding documents that 'shall not be abridged'.

Yet, we have a mental illness issue in this country. You can make statistics show that there is a great increase in mass shootings in the last couple decades, or you can make them show none. ('there are three kinds of lies: lies, damned lies, and statistics', attribution unclear)

Among the several states, there are levels of gun control from extreme (Massachusetts and California) to few or none (Vermont, Texas). The statistics I look at show a correlation between tight restrictions and violence. This is similar to the black market we talked about with prohibitions. The cities with the most restrictions have higher gun violence rates. Chicago and Illinois have some of the most stringent laws, but the violence rates far exceed averages. It's a self-perpetuating 'chicken or egg' scenario.

I repeat this often: Prohibition never works.

However, there may need to be a way of restricting weapons from those that exhibit mental illness and the mechanisms and thresholds to regulate it from improper use. This deserves debate and consideration from all sides to find compromise, but it must be done in an intellectually honest way without the fallacy and dishonest language we've talked about at length thus far.

Politicizing tragic events is not a legitimate way of starting a discussion. After the 2019 shooting in a Virginia municipal building, Governor Northam proposed a string of new restrictions. As terrible a situation as this was, an employee who seemingly cracked out of the blue, this was such a cynical, opportunistic action.

None of the proposed new restrictions would have stopped the suspect in this case. If this shooting had exposed a way of stopping such an act then it might be less obscene to use the grief so blatantly but taking such political advantage for a red herring is disgusting. It certainly had taken the media off the scent of his blackface scandal.

We can find ways to discuss sensitive issues being respectful, empathetic and understanding that we must all get along.

Common Ground

We've spent some (digital) ink exploring what ails us and what is making us all so testy. We looked at an introduction to Libertarians and the range of views they hold. Also, why I think a centrist libertarian view is the only way to save our country from the division and debt laden path we're on.

So, let's take a look at where we have common ground with each other; right, left, north.

The hardest part of making this comparison, and why I'll keep this brief, is because action and philosophy change depending on who is in power. These comparisons are therefore a moving target and are terribly inconsistent. Republicans are really anti-government when the democrats are in power, but when they get the checkbook, that changes.

The same changes can be found on the left. Nancy Pelosi is railing against spending and tax cuts as proposed by Trump, but was ok with deficit spending when Obama proposed it. This goes back to creating the artificial divisiveness that we've discussed, and to the need to pay off supporters once in power.

The view I take below is what the mainstream members seem to think and what the platforms are based on.

Right:

The right and north common ground (in theory) is in appreciating small government and free markets. Unfortunately, this hasn't been coming out in practice as the Republicans held congress and the White House for President Trump's first two years. Government did not shrink like the right would have led you to think it should under a Republican administration. It actually grew considerably along with the deficit.

The deficit for 2020 fiscal year is projected to be almost a trillion dollars. So that's just not working out. It seems that whichever party is in power complains about spending until they're in power and then they want spending on everything they want.

How about free markets? Republicans are more free market than the Democrats and left. However, like spending, it crumbles once they're in power. Tariffs are the least free trade thing a country can impose, yet...

Left:

Libertarian common ground with the left centers around social freedoms and tolerance. Again, the common ground stands in philosophy until you get to practice.

Libertarians have generally been for same sex marriage, for LGBTQ equal rights, and racial equality since its founding in the early 1970s. It's part of the philosophy that you should be able to do what you wish as long as you don't infringe on the rights of someone else.

We part ways in that last clause, 'as long as you don't infringe on the rights of someone else'. In practice, the left is open to using force to compel other people to violate their own views.

In Colorado, a baker is now being sued for a third time, despite prevailing the first at the Supreme Court, by left activists because he refused to create a custom cake for a gay wedding. His bakery is open to the public and as a public accommodation he has never discriminated against anyone who wished to buy something off the shelf.

However, he declined to create a custom wedding cake because it would violate his religious views. The supreme court determined that Masterpiece Cake's religious views were not respected. The owner said, "a wedding cake is an inherently religious event and the cake is definitely a specific message".

So where is the tolerance the left wants? They only demand tolerance when it's to their agenda. When it's tolerance to someone else's, it's offensive.

Center:

Go back and look at the 'Greene – Fogg Curve' in the section 'division creates power' and remember that most people are not dyed-in-the-wool anything.

A Practical Libertarian

They're victims of the politics of division and follow the party that guilts them the most.

Rather than espousing a left government or a right government, the message I want you to take away is <u>*neither side should be using government in this way*</u>. As long as we do, we will seesaw our way into oblivion trying to outdo, outspend, out guilt each other.

Using the threat of violence to promote your agenda to the detriment of others is the problem. This tactic is used by both sides.

Victimless 'crimes', business licensing, 'special' rights instead of equal rights, these are all signs of a government and political environment gone amuck.

Government shouldn't be giving anyone privileges, it shouldn't be protecting us from ourselves, it shouldn't be giving us rights (we have those already!).

The weight of crushing debt and unfunded commitments, of special interests, of unjust taxation, of intrusiveness and spying, of increasing government interest in our daily lives will be our undoing.

We won't fully recognize our freedoms and get back to the prosperity that we had until we break this cycle of rotating self-aggrandizement.

It's ok if we're different. Let's celebrate it and not let each other capitalize on it. We must give each other the room to be different with a modicum of respect.

Practical Steps to do Today to Start Turning the Ship

"In a revolution, as in a novel, the most difficult part to invent is the end" -- Alexis De Tocqueville

We live in a multi-cultural, multi-politic, multi-religion, multi-everything country. It is imperative that we find ways to come together to fix all the broken things discussed so far.

It behooves us to direct the evolution of the United States Government to one that respects its citizens and respects the spirit of liberties under which it was formed. Writing for FEE, Barry Brownstein wrote, "Virtue begins when we want the same freedom for others that we want for ourselves".[39]

I want you to have the same freedoms. I want you and I, both, to be able to live our best lives as we each see fit.

We can start by limiting the artificial division that politicians have produced.

To do that we need to start with some points of agreement:

Have Ground Rules

We need to have some serious discussions where people listen to each other to find common ground.

-- If we're going to have a discussion that does it's best to avoid artificial division:

-- If we're going to have a discussion that does it's best to lean on (actual) facts (and not 'alternative facts'):

-- If we're going to have a discussion that encourages interaction and finding of common ground:

---

[39] https://fee.org/articles/why-it-must-be-the-people-who-preserve-the-flame-of-liberty/

Then, we need to start with some ground rules.

1. Discussion needs to be based on facts, not conjecture or good intentions.
2. Discussions include ALL facts, not just those that are convenient to one's viewpoint. Intentional omission is as bad as misrepresentation.
3. Facts have no person, so no personal (ad-hominin) attacks. If the facts don't support your position, then maybe you should change your opinion.
4. Declare opinion: opinion on interpreting facts is necessary, but you must declare where fact ends and opinion begins - therefore any 'adjustments', seasonal or otherwise, are to be declared clearly. "Given these facts, therefore, it is my opinion…"
5. No baseline budgeting. A cut is a reduction compared to today or the year being compared to. A 'flat' budget that includes increases isn't flat, helps to hide spending, and allows distortive language to detract from facts. Facts cannot be based on assumptions, which are what drive baseline budgets.
6. All accounting must be subject to GAAP standards, and that includes *all* government spending. We can't make judgements about the effectiveness of government if we don't have confidence in facts. Generally Accepted Accounting Principles (GAAP) are a good starting point to lending credibility.
7. All agencies – governmental, quasi-governmental and government sponsored enterprises - must be subject to regular, frequent audits of their books.
8. There can be no hidden budgets for secret programs. There can be a single line item rolled up for all black programs included in the public budget. Accounting for the programs included in that roll-up follow the same rules, and though the line items may be hidden from the public, performance must be reported. It is imperative that the full cost of government be transparent so the People can determine its effectiveness and prevent graft. The concept of 'off-budget' is counter to a government that can be overseen by its people. Anything spent, traded, or expended must be in the public budget.

Respect Opinion

Opinion is important – it differentiates how we view the same facts. It differentiates things by valuing our personal sense of importance.

Opinion is interesting. A recent survey on education showed that 35 percent of 8th graders could read at a proficient or higher level. There were two reactions... one about how appalling the number was that only a third could read with proficiency. The other was 'Wow, that's awesome! It went up from 29 percent 10 years ago!'. Same facts, different reaction and opinion.

If we understand the same set of facts and how people's personal history shapes their opinions, it's easier to be empathetic. Wwhen we have empathy we can determine just how best to find compromise.

Separate People from Corporations

In the 2012 Presidential election, Mitt Romney said at a rally in Iowa that 'Corporations are people'.

Wikipedia defines 'corporate personhood' as "the legal notion that a corporation, separately from its associated human beings (like owners, managers, or employees), has at least some of the legal rights and responsibilities enjoyed by natural persons (physical humans)"

We need to separate corporations from people (personhood).

The idea of allowing corporations to take financial and product risks necessary to do well in the market sounds good. It is important that personal and professional liability have some distance to allow that. But, we've created an idea that a corporation can do bad without bringing to justice the people behind the corporation who did the directing.

His follow up statement showed that even with his experience and degrees, he didn't fully understand the dichotomy of what this means. Romney said, 'Everything corporations earn ultimately goes to people.' And this is why we need to place them in their own category. Corporations pass on everything they do to people; you could call them a 'pass through entity' to steal a tax term.

Corporations can't skip meals if their financials are poor, they don't splurge on new clothes in good times, they don't feel sad when they do poorly.

Everything a corporation does affects someone. In lean times a corporation's bad performance is passed through to one of three groups: It affects the corporation's employees with lower wages or layoffs, it affects the corporation's customers in the form of higher prices or lower quality products, or the stock holders in lower returns. The opposite is true as well, in better wages, competitive pricing (or better products) or improved dividends. At no time does the 'corporation' care. If the corporation erects a fancy new building, it's the employees who benefit. The 'corporation' doesn't care.

By de-linking personhood we can correctly pass-through the big item of concern: criminal liability. People in corporations make decisions that lead to polluting, to dangerous products, to fraud. There is much moral hazard in isolating the decisions that drive a corporation and the liability of the corporation itself.

We previously mentioned the Lehman scandal in 2007 and the surrounding failures of that economic crisis. Despite some corporate fines and several bankruptcies, there were never any executives that were held accountable for the decisions they made in allowing the corporations they ran to do illegal and improper things like misrepresent the ratings of a bond issue.

Government support for corporations can also be interpreted as graft. Grants to Solyndra, a solar panel company, padded a lot of pockets and boosted the pay of a lot of executives and bankers who facilitated the 500 million dollar guaranteed loan. Solyndra's run lasted only two years, a pretty spectacular burn rate for half a billion dollars of the People's money.

The Inspector General's report on the scandal says "The actions of certain Solyndra officials were, at best, reckless and irresponsible or, at worst, an orchestrated effort to knowingly and intentionally deceive and mislead the Department." Again, no criminal charges were ever brought.

Implement the 'Fair Tax'

The Fair Tax is a solution based on spending and not on income. Unlike the IRS, which requires reporting of our income and investment activities (and the audits that come with such intrusion), this tax is based on spending. It is enforced by the states as part of their existing sales tax infrastructures (48 of 50) and they will keep a share to pay the costs of the required growth. Aside from telling the government where to send your rebate there is no government interference in your personal lives.

The Fair Tax is 100% progressive to the poverty line. This means that anyone with income at or below the poverty line will pay nothing in taxes. This is made possible by refunding the tax on poverty level spending (pre-funded in advance) to everyone.

There are countless advantages to this system, and it has been studied more than any other alternative.

- The Fair Tax replaces ALL payroll-based taxes including Social Security and Medicare.
- The Fair Tax replaces ALL corporate taxes.
- The Fair Tax expands the tax base by taxing tourists and immigrants/ visitors/ undocumented people regardless of status.
- Our exports become more attractive because the income tax portion of their cost is eliminated. Like the imports that come to us without their home country's VAT (value added tax), our products will be more competitive on a flat playing field overseas.
- Income from US company foreign activities comes back to our shores freely because it is not taxed at the border.
- You can choose to live near tax free if you buy used items. The Fair Tax only applies to new products, and services.
- There are no special interests. Products and services are taxed equally for everyone.

That last item is why there is much opposition to this, and yet, this is by design and a one of the best features of the plan. A large percentage of the lobby groups in Washington are there to push for special rules for their industry in the tax code. Government officials don't want to sacrifice the money and power they wield when they are given money for a cause.

The FairTax removes incentives for special treatment in the tax code. Everyone is treated equally.

What the Fair Tax does is replace the IRS and all income-based taxes with a like amount of income from a sales tax. It is a one-for-one replacement. It does not make judgements about spending, programs, or any other changes. Those would need to come separately.

From a business perspective, it is similarly advantageous. The idea of tax planning being strategic in how you spend on infrastructure or capital items goes away. You report sales in the aggregate and pay the tax that you marked up. It's very matter of fact and simple to account for. You don't 'turn in' your customers by providing the government 1099s.

The government has no reason to know how you're spending your income. If you spend on travel and meals, if you spend on operating expense versus capital expense is up to you and what you want to get out of your business. Your tax bill requires no planning, no tax attorneys. Account for what makes your business great, not what makes Government happy (and how that's going to change every 4 or 8 years).

Detractors will complain that the tax percentage is too high. They employ methods that are a bit deceptive. It's a red herring. When we compare rates to the income tax we use an inclusive rate. The inclusive rate of the Fair Tax is 23%. While this sounds high, remember that the cost of all the employment and corporate taxes come out of the cost of the item so untaxed prices on most items are expected to drop at least by the tax. On your paystub Social Security and Medicare are 7.5%, your employer pays a matching 7.5%, plus your income tax rate which marginally is up to 33%.

The inclusive tax rate is quoted to compare it to income taxes which are also an inclusive rate. For every $100 in income, the government keeps $23. A 23% tax rate.

The deception is comparing income tax 'inclusive' rates to the 'exclusive' tax rate. At the sales counter in most states you see a price and then add the tax, it's not already embedded. So, if you buy a $77 dollar item the total would be $100. Calculated in this additive method instead of subtractive, the rate is 30% even though you've paid the same in real dollars.[40]

Either way the tax paid is the same. If we make current tax tables exclusive instead of inclusive, the 24% tax rate becomes 31.5% and that's before Social Security & Medicare.

---

[40] Please visit FairTax.org, they do a more elegant job of describing this.

There are several entire books on the topic of the FairTax so I'll spare the details here, but they are well worth the read. I'll put a link to the FairTax website in the conclusion at the end of this book.

Fix Immigration

There are few topics as divisive as immigration. This area is full of inflammatory and misleading information so let's apply the ground rules and see where we should start.

Let's start working from some common definitions that I've written up:

To me...

- An immigrant is a person in the United States legally who came from another country, and who has a status that allows them to stay and gain employment.
- An immigrant may be here on an H1 visa, for example, have a green card, or have naturalized and become a citizen.
- Visitors or tourists are people who are here legally but their status only allows them to stay temporarily and they cannot gain employment legally.
- Those who are here with no legal status are not immigrants, they are undocumented and as such are violating either the civil code, immigration law or both.

There are many conversational pitfalls that have been deployed by the mainstream parties to weaponize discussion of this topic. The use of terms like 'illegal' for 'undocumented' is one of them. However, keep in mind the realities of law.

It IS against the law for a non-citizen to be in the United States without documentation showing what privileges they have. Those documents could be a visitor visa, a green card, or a work permit. Each gives privilege – some to travel, some to be employed for a particular employer for a set amount of time, some to remain resident in the US without restriction. It is also against the law to cross into the United States without using a proper checkpoint.

There are semantics involved around whether breaking those laws is a criminal offense or civil violation (deportation is considered a civil penalty), but it violates

A Practical Libertarian

law and that argument is really a distraction. Whether you've committed a crime or a violation is irrelevant to the outcome.

Regardless of whether it's a civil violation to not have documentation, it is a crime to have overstayed a visa or cross the border without going through a checkpoint and that covers a vast majority of offenders in that situation, which is the second part of why the argument is diversionary on its face.

In discussing this, I've heard much clamor about whether this is right or not, but we cannot start the discussion without standardizing our language and starting point. This is the policy and law today, regardless of how you think it *should* be.

The Libertarian position on immigration is that it should be pretty open. How open depends on where you fall on the spectrum with most anarchists believing in no border controls.

My viewpoint, A Practical Libertarian, is yes, we should do background checks at the border and make sure entrants have appropriate identification and aren't on criminal offender lists. Yes, we need barriers that force people to enter through our front door. That is part of the government's duty to keep us safe. However, it should be much easier for people to come and work, and come and go as they please.

The Encyclopedia of Libertarianism presents the viewpoint well: "Efforts by the government to manage the labor market are as apt to fail as similar efforts to protect domestic industries or orchestrate industrial policy. [...] If an immigrant seeks to engage in peaceful, voluntary transactions that do not threaten the freedom or security of the native-born, the government should not interfere."[41]

There still should be different levels of entry. Tourist entry can have lower barriers than people that wish to come and stay. But we need to enforce those laws when they stay too long and become undocumented.

It is sad and makes for a heart wrenching human interest story when someone undocumented is removed from the US after having been here for a long time. While I think it should be easier for people to come and work, we need to enforce the laws they have broken.

---

41 The Encyclopedia of Libertarianism. Thousand Oaks, California: SAGE Publications, Cato Institute

When it comes to DACA and those referred to as the 'dreamers' (people who were brought here through no fault of their own as minors and remain undocumented as adults) we need to accommodate them. While they are technically in violation of the law, they are not the ones who violated it. Their parents or custodians did.

This needs to be codified in law, lawfully, not through presidential decree under questionable authority. The rhetoric on both sides of this issue is too inflammatory to be left to interpretation. It is worth doing, and doing so in a manner that dots the 'i's and crosses the 't's.

One thing we can do to discourage illegal entry is modify the birthright citizenship. Currently, under the constitution, anyone who is born on American soil is automatically an American citizen. With the election of President Trump and his anti-immigration policies this has had quite a bit of discussion, but it's centered around an all-or-nothing approach.

I believe there is middle ground, understanding it would take a constitutional amendment to achieve. The middle ground is that anyone born on American soil is a citizen when their parents are citizens OR reside here legally with a permit or visa that allows for work.

This takes away the incentive for people to come to give birth as tourists (American citizenship is valuable!) or crossing the border illegally. This is middle ground that I think we can compromise on and addresses the ills.

Medical Bill of Rights

There is a distinct disconnect between medical practice, medicine, and patients where costs are concerned. I suspect that this came about in large part because of regulation around insurance. Insurance companies have large lobbying budgets. They've managed to evolve our system to one where every dollar gets funneled through one of their companies or Medicare/Medicaid.

According to the Center for Responsive Politics, lobbying in the healthcare sector in 2018 was over $565 million dollars.[42] With 535 people in Congress... well let's just say it sound excessive.

---

42 https://www.opensecrets.org/lobby/indus.php?id=H&year=2018

A Practical Libertarian

We accept practices in health care that we don't allow anywhere else in society. For example, The Federal Trade Commission Act makes it a 'deceptive practice' to label a sale item as a percent off discount from a price it never sold at. Yet, at hospitals there is something called a Charge Master that lists 'retail prices' for their services. The only people that 'might' actually pay those are uninsured and people not savvy enough to ask for insurance pricing.

In 2013 the Centers for Medicare and Medicaid Services (CMS) first publicly released some of the Charge Master details. Forbes commented on the resulting analysis, "What emerges through a preliminary analysis is a snapshot of an incoherent system in which prices for critical medical services vary seemingly at random — from state to state, region to region and hospital to hospital."[43]

While this has improved in small ways with the details becoming public, the public are still systematically isolated from the cost of care. With health insurance, most people only see relatively small copays, and small hospital deductibles. They have no incentive to be competitive shoppers like they are with almost all other commodity services and products.

Think of any other product or service... we might get a discount for cash or upfront payment. When we finance things, there is usually a kickback to the seller with a portion of the interest. Car dealers are very convincing that you use their financing, aren't they?

We need a 'redo'. We need to reconnect pricing to costs and the best way to do this is to implement absolute transparency: Transparency in the Government and practitioner's lobby to know who is padding politician's and practitioner's pockets, transparency in what insurance companies pay for care on our behalf, transparency in what things actually cost, and transparency in what insurance costs us all.

I mentioned earlier that the free market was the most efficient arbiter of prices and product availability. We have sucked so much of the free out of this market that the self-regulating aspects have disappeared.

A Medical Bill of Rights. Not to be confused with the 'patient bill of rights' that President Obama announced in 2010: That mandated a lot of expensive things like eliminating the pre-existing condition clauses in many policies, eliminating lifetime caps on policies and protecting our choice of doctors (we all know how that worked

---

[43] https://www.huffpost.com/entry/hospital-prices-cost-differences_n_3232678?1367985666=

out in Obama's 'Affordable Care Act'). It didn't do anything to fix the system beyond demanding more coverage.

Again, don't confuse disagreement with the tactic as disagreement with the outcome.

A redo must start by removing barriers to competition like allowing inter-state insurance companies.

It must continue with allowing purchasing groups that aren't employer based. If an employer wants to provide money towards a plan and offer their own that's great, but it shouldn't prevent me from going into a group plan with people from a church group, or AARP, or any other that we may desire.

It should contain mandatory reporting on what is paid on your behalf.

Medical Savings Accounts would be a great idea if we hadn't already talked about eliminating the income tax (since ALL our income should be tax free!). Despite the furor over the high deductibles, it is a good way to reconnect people with what they're paying by making them write a check.

Several years ago, the company I worked for put in a high deductible plan. The HR Manager apologized for the increased deductible despite the price going down by an equal amount. I stood and thanked her. I told her that what she had just done was take that money out of the hands of the insurance company and put it back in our control.

We should also have a frank discussion about the merits (or lack of) of Cadillac coverage vs the old fashioned 'hospital plan' or 'catastrophic care plan'. People are far more likely to go to see doctors for every minor ache and scratch when they only have a small copay.

Doesn't it make more sense that I pay for the routine out of pocket? And, like my auto collision coverage and extended warranty that don't cover brakes and oil changes, I'm covered for anything out of the ordinary.

Campaign Finance Reform

Right now, we have incoherent systems of election finance laws. They differ depending on whether you're running for a House seat, the Senate, state office, or local office. They also differ depending on who you are or represent.

If you support a candidate but want to give more than the limit then you can start a Political Action Committee. There are other 'committees' as well. Some have protected donor lists, some don't. Some can collect donations from corporations, some not.

Some are regulated at the state level with onerous restrictions. For example, in Florida you cannot put out a change jar for small donations. You need to collect donor information that includes their employer for any donation. But if the candidate is running for US Senate you can collect up to $50 anonymously. If you have a party table at a park or 4th of July event you have to track what is donated to the party, separately from what is donated to any candidates, federal, state or local.

Going back to the transparency rules we talked about in Medical reform, let's make this transparent and remove the restrictions. Politicians can accept donations from PEOPLE, (not corporations or any artificial 'personhood') and those donor lists are made public with donations under $100 exempt. Donations must be made directly and re-bundling, or middle man redistribution is not allowed.

Corporations cannot donate directly, though with no income tax (See FairTax above) we would have no care if a corporation gave employees money to donate. Let watchdog groups police who is giving to who.

Then, encourage state and local governments to adopt the same rules to simplify running for office.

Many have suggested that politicians wear the logos of their supporters NASCAR style. So many, in fact, that I tried to find specific attribution and couldn't among the 980,000 results on Google. I like this idea as it would be a timely reminder that elections are expensive. As part of running, politicians become beholden, even if only unconsciously.

Enact Election Reform

While we're on the topic of campaigns and elections… let's talk about how our elected officials concentrate power, and equity.

Clarify Pseudo-Elections

Did you realize primaries, most notably for President because of their notoriety, are not actually public elections? They are the apparatus of how the parties nominate their candidate for the actual election in November. This is why some states have caucuses, some elections and some both. The result of the election is an elector who then votes at the party convention (except California's top-two elections).

This is also why the primary dates vary so much. This process was not defined in the constitution, but by the parties.

This presents two issues. Timing and participation.

We need to refine the purpose of primaries and either revert them to the parties to run, or standardize and federalize them. It's an equal protection issue to me as votes in Iowa don't count the same way votes in California do with a top-two primary system. By putting what looks like a government stamp on them by polling them where we have ACTUAL elections, we deceive people as to how their votes count or don't.

In 'open primary' states like Massachusetts, you can decide at the poll which party you wish to vote under. If I'm registered as a Democrat, why should I be allowed to meddle in the Republican primary? Good question, I don't know.

The presidential primary, specifically, has a date problem as well. The race to vote first is absurd and has only served to extend the election cycle to where it's almost perpetual. One election ends and we're already talking about who's going to beat the scoundrel that got in, next time.

It may be time to federalize the primaries for equity, both in dropping the 'race to vote first' and in standardizing who has rights to participate. I'm sure there's a lot of unexplored discussion to be had on this matter and I look forward to hearing the viewpoints.

Level Power

Our elected officials are swayed by election donors whether they do it consciously or not. The longer someone is in office, and the more power they wield because of their seniority, the easier it is to get reelection funding and it perpetuates a vicious cycle.

We should consider term limits for our federal officials. Congress has failed to manage itself in an equitable way and that gives people represented by 'powerful' representatives and senators more clout than others.

Seniority in Congress sets up long rivalries and discourages work across the aisle. It sets up Congress as a ruling class. Chairmanships are given to those who have been there the longest, instead of those best suited to the committee.

This will be a tough sell. It will need to be passed by Congress, and they're not likely to vote themselves out of a job without overwhelming popular support.

Have a Legal Do-over

We should expire the US Code. Give Congress 5 or 10 years to replace it and pass new law from scratch. At the current size it's too big, too dated, too special interest laden to fix.

We start by ignoring regulating activities that have no victim. That's a good start... if no one's rights are violated, if no one is hurt other than, perhaps, the person doing the activity, then it should not be illegal. Government is not a parent, it's not a nanny. We should be responsible for ourselves.

We let the laws that give constituencies special privilege expire. No one should get special treatment in the tax code. If the tax is onerous then it's onerous for everyone. The government should not be picking winners and losers regardless of whether it is for good intent or a well-funded constituent.

We let the laws expire that restrict action based on certain group's morals. Government should stay out of our bedrooms, dining rooms, and living rooms. If you don't like something that someone else is doing, don't do it.

We continue by annotating every new law passed with the clause in the constitution that authorizes it.

What we'll end up with is an economy and population that is much more nimble, more aware of boundaries and more likely to respect the law. We unleash the creativity that comes with freedom.

We also end up with people that are more responsible because there's no excuse that Government should have stopped you from being stupid.

When the country sees how well that works, each state should do the same: Expire their code of regulations and start from scratch with these same guidelines.

Conclusion

I mentioned writing this book to a friend and he remarked "I didn't know you were an author!". I LOLd, out loud! I told him this will be considered a hobby until I sell a thousand copies. That will earn me the title.

The fact is, I'm not yet an author. I'm not a politician. I'm just an average Jim, who along with everyone I know, is beyond frustrated and angry with the state of our politics and government.

I've worked on again and off again with the Libertarian Party in Florida and have been frustrated with lack of foresight, misunderstanding of macro politics and a focus on irrelevant minutiae that prevents any kind of coordinated action. I've not been active in the National Party, but am similarly frustrated from afar by its inability to come together.

They're really good at getting ballot access, and sadly, that in and of itself is a feat. But fielding candidates? There's a quadrennial argument about funding presidential campaigns and who owns donor lists. They have not shown me they are worthy of my donation or time with a convincing appeal that they can act as anything more than a club.

The suggestions I make here are based on what I think are common sense. I don't see this anywhere else; I hope you read it and are inspired to act. Without action this is all for naught.

I hope that this book can be a first step, a conversation starter. If we can get a movement going that will pick some of my suggestions to incorporate transparency, honesty, empathy and stop forcing personal agendas on everyone else then this will have been worthwhile.

I'm grateful for my family that helped edit this, and who challenge my political thinking daily.

I cannot conclude without calling out some resources that I DO follow and find worthwhile. They walk the walk and I'm grateful for them:

A Practical Libertarian

FEE, the Foundation for Economic Education. FEE.org

> *"FEE's mission is to inspire, educate, and connect future leaders with the economic, ethical, and legal principles of a free society.*
> *These principles include: individual liberty, free-market economics, entrepreneurship, private property, high moral character, and limited government."*

The CATO Institute. CATO.org

> *"The Cato Institute is a public policy research organization — a think tank — dedicated to the principles of individual liberty, limited government, free markets, and peace."*

The FairTax, and Americans for Fair Taxation (AFFT). FairTax.org

> *"AFFT began as a research organization. Extensive polling and focus group studies were commissioned with a financially, ethnically and politically diverse group of taxpayers. The results of these studies led to a nonpartisan team of economists who developed the FairTax® plan."*

Reason Foundation. Reason.org

> *"Reason Foundation advances a free society by developing, applying, and promoting libertarian principles, including individual liberty, free markets, and the rule of law.*

> *"Reason Foundation produces respected public policy research on a variety of issues and publishes the critically-acclaimed Reason magazine. Together, our top-tier think tank and political and cultural magazine reach a diverse, influential audience, advancing the values of choice, individual freedom and limited government."*

Notes:

Notes:

Notes:

Made in the USA
Middletown, DE
21 July 2019